Beautiful Sadness

Joy Jennings

IN YOUR FACE INK, LLC

Glendale, AZ   ·   2008

In Your Face Ink LLC
9524 W. Camelback Road
#130-182
Glendale, AZ 85305
Tel: (623) 570-1072
www.inyourfaceink.com

Printed in the United States of America
First Printing: November 2008
ISBN 0-9765659-3-5
Library of Congress Control Number on file.
Jennings, Joy
Beautiful Sadness

Design and Typesetting: Edward J. Kamholz
Cover photograph: Shutterstock
Joy Jennings' photograph: Dawn Manikunian

Blessings always!
Joy Jennings

Beautiful Sadness

The Journey of Hope and Compassion Through Life and Loss

Joy Jennings

For my children, Ellen, Carol, and Bruce, who experienced the loss of so many loved ones in their early childhood years. Your tender caring hearts helped me stay focused on life and love despite the many losses in our lives; you helped me heal and started the journey that led to this book.

Acknowledgements

No book is written in a vacuum. I am blessed with the loving support of many extraordinary people who have helped and I wish to thank them. The first and most special thank you belongs to Melanie Stronach, who saw my writing in its original and very raw form. She saw the potential and guided me with wisdom laced with kindness. Mel became my guiding light. This book represents her faith in my stories, many versions down the line, and could not have materialized without her patience and pivotal input.

My computer help began with the gift of one from Pierre de Serres. Bruce Mole had the considerable task of teaching me basics of computer use and straightening out my disasters whenever I was on the West Coast writing. Back East, I am forever indebted to Bob Reynolds, who saw me through computer crashes and solved problems whenever I called…and that was often. These people are my heroes.

Beyond that I am indebted to Diane McAllister, Gwen Bardo, and Brenda Howard for their unfailing encouragement from the start of my writing. Jan Archer, Caroline Boddie, Diane Jessop, Barb Baker, Kate Hanlon, Cathyrn Bond Doyle, and Rosemary Markham provided ongoing and magical support that helped me endure. A very special thank you goes to Patti Cody for her ongoing cheerleading, feedback, professional advice, and non-stop push to help me realize my dream. Likewise a special thank you to Gladys

Morrison, who provided my southern writing place and helped me continue to progress. Shirley Verhoorn was a source of technical information and inspiration. Frank Asch became a mentor, who provided sound advice, intermittent feedback and was an ongoing source of strength. His joy at my progress has been a source of pride for me and I thank him for all of that. My daughters, Ellen Mole and Carol McKee, helped in creative and important ways. Additional sources of encouragement include: Jill Price, Irene Yaychuk Arabai, Audrey Barker, Emily Ryckman, Gerri Knight, Jan de Serres, Kerri Gardner, AJ Hauser, Cynthia Felleisen, Monica Palko, Barbara Eder, Patti Hyman, Tom Orloski, Ellen Degraad, Crystal Crews, Dr.Ismael Olivares, Steve Barish, Ric Warren, Dr. Gary Arthur, and all who continued to ask about my book. All of these became my nuts-and-bolts support team who fueled my determination and helped fan my dreams into reality.

My most important thank you is to express my gratitude to the wonderful patients and families who opened their lives, their hearts, thoughts, and hopes to me. My time with them shaped and changed my life, and my very awareness of just how precious life and relationships with others are in our brief time here. They became my teachers and gifted my life beyond ability to put into words. These stories are a tribute to their courage.

I will always be grateful to Laura Browne and Jill Ferguson, my editors and publishers, who believed in these stories and turned my dream into reality. Their support and wise counsel has been a gift in itself, and I thank them from my heart.

To my readers, thank you for opening your hearts to the wonderful stories of these teachers and letting yourself be guided and healed by their valuable insights. In so doing their lives and wisdom live on, and the gift of giving continues.

Beautiful Sadness

Introduction

Life has a way of presenting the unexpected, even the unthinkable, and in a blink events beyond one's worst fears can unfold. Such was the case when I was in my early thirties, with three young children. I lost my brother, father, and mother in seventeen months. My mother, the last of the three to die, did so suddenly two days after I had assumed care of my mother-in-law, whom we had found on the floor in need of immediate help.

Experiencing the unthinkable taught me many lessons. I had no choice but to face it. Death in that close succession cannot be ignored. Denial, sealing over my feelings, rising above it and carrying on bravely, (all coping plans our current society enthusiastically embraces), failed to work when tragedy kept speeding at me like an out of control freight train. I would have preferred to escape, but there was no place to run.

Eventually I learned I was much stronger than I thought possible. The strength was interlaced with episodes of overwhelming belief that I couldn't survive, that I was going crazy and never would feel happy and safe again. I felt old as soon as I lived to be older than my brother, and it took some ferreting out to recognize that I felt displaced guilt at living longer than he did. I didn't have the right to be living and enjoying myself when he was gone.

Ultimately, experiencing the unthinkable taught me that no matter what else death is, it is a gift that teaches us about life, and it challenges us to make what we can from every precious part of the time that we have.

Time has led me to believe there is no death, only life in different places. At seventeen, when I began nurse's training, I feared catastrophe and death. I wanted to find out how to deal with those parts of life that come without choice or warning. Now, I have come to a firm conviction that death is a highly under-rated, beautiful experience that has received bad press. I know my loved ones still exist, for I can feel their presence. This knowledge springs from a place within I have come to recognize as my place of knowing. The journey between those two points of view has not been dull.

I was not alone on this journey. Along the way I had the help and understanding of loving friends and family. I found solace in the writings of others from across the ages. The wonderful unseen forces that sustain the universe were there to draw upon. I had but to ask in prayer.

Love for my children and from them, was a stabilizing force and incredible blessing that helped me choose to find a way through my grief, and to learn to invest in life again, fully and joyfully. The question, "Aren't we ever going to be happy again?" fueled my conviction to find the way.

One of the incredible gifts I received is to learn that we survive grief because we choose to. Amid the conviction we don't know how, choosing to find a way can open doors that lead us out of the sorrow engulfing all aspects of our lives.

I found I was drawn to help others experiencing grief, for when we help others we help ourselves. It's as if all that loss leads, at last, to something positive we can value: the ability to bring comfort to ease others' grief.

Through assisting others, I uncovered another truth of living. Incredible forces can unfold, when we sit and hold the energy with love and caring for others to just be and grow, as they work through the challenges and stages forced by impending death. Others can and do grow, free of judgement and criticism, and supported by the rich and limitless power of love. One of life's paradoxes unfolds. Sitting and holding the energy doesn't feel like nearly enough to give, and it is everything to receive.

It has become a choice from my heart to care for those who face death, to reach out in love and support to them. I have received infinitely more than I have given.

It was years later I began receiving a poem during meditation, seemingly out of nowhere, without premonition.

Talk to me softly, I need the sound of your voice,
To weld me to reality before I face the night.
Talk to me softly, it matters not what you say.
Just talk to me lovingly that I may face the day.
Talk to me softly, talk to me with your hands.
Your touch so warm and gentle tells me you understand.
But talk to me sparingly, my strength is ebbing away.
Talk to me lovingly. I must face the day.

I've written a poem! I thought. I wonder why? What does this mean? Eventually I knew it meant I was to write a book about dying, how to talk with others at this highly crucial time and to share the wonderful gifts of understanding my patients had given. I have seen many dimensions of death since then, studied people's reactions, attended multiple conferences, listened to survivors, and pondered the meaning of death and grief. My conviction that pain shared is more easily borne became unshakable.

As I grew through the experiences of my beautiful patients, this book found its form. My patients' stories share different aspects of the journey from life to death. I prefer to think the journey is from life to another phase of life we happen to call death.

Beautiful Sadness is equally about the beauty of healing the heart, achieved through facing life's transitions and challenges. Our hearts can heal, by learning from the insights and wisdom grief offers, by completing the journey with hope, courage, and compassion.

It is an honor to be with someone when he is dying. I feel deeply honored to have known the people in these stories, who openly shared their hopes, dreams, fears, insights and who they are with me. They have enriched my life beyond what words convey. You are about to meet these very real people, with names and facts changed to protect their privacy. I have worked to preserve the essence and integrity of their being and the magical events that were set in motion by their commitment to live life fully until they died. I share them with you now, that your life may also be graced by their courage, strength, and healing insights. Their wonderful legacies live on in the hearts of all who listen. May the beautiful gifts they gave me be yours to share and call your own.

Journey

Let me tell you the secret that has led me to my goal:
my strength lies solely in my tenacity.

~ Louis Pasteur

The train whistle blew a melodic but insistent sound warning motorists waiting reluctantly at the crossroads as the Coast Starlight rounded the bend. I was in California visiting my children and working on my book, and I had succumbed to the allure of a romantic train ride to see our country's magnificent coastline. The magic began with the "All aboard" and the first blow of the whistle. Now, for a moment with a smile on my face, as I settled into my seat, I could sense the charm that holds captive train lovers everywhere.

I adjusted the seat back to view the terrain, and with the thrill of seeing a part of the world never before witnessed by my eyes, suddenly, I understood the allure of the railroads.

That reminded me of Andy. How could I ride a train and not think of Andy? I met Andy when his doctor had referred him to home care while having yet another round of cancer treatments. His blood counts had plummeted, and my directions were to open his case and check him for

signs of infection, and assess his needs, his ability to function at home, and his response to the latest round of
chemotherapy.

When I got to Andy's, trains greeted me as soon as I
opened the door. Memorabilia filled the rooms of the
apartment where Andy, thin and pale and looking more
than a little anxious, sat in a recliner. Photos covered the
walls, pictures of a proud Andy standing straight and tall in
his uniform and cap by his latest train assignment, photos
of Andy receiving awards for outstanding work on the railroads, and photos of many of the renowned trains of our
country's early history, streaking proudly across the USA.
Andy could name every one of them.

I sat down in the closest chair. "Let me turn on the light
for you," he said, as he switched on the perfect replica of an
engineer's lantern. He smiled shyly, as he let the switch
pause a moment on red, then chose instead the usual soft
light for the room while watching my reaction.

We began where it always begins, with introductions.
"I'm Joy, your homecare nurse. It's nice to meet you."

"Nice to meet you too, Nurse, but I won't be needing to
see much of you. I'm just fine, and I can't think of a thing I
could need from homecare."

I smiled. That had a familiar ring especially from my male
patients. Accustomed as they are, to carrying on no matter
how they felt, they far preferred to see themselves as caretakers rather than recipients of someone else's efforts. "Well,
it won't hurt to open your case anyway, Andy. May I call you
Andy?" As he nodded, I added, "Homecare nurses can
sometimes spot little things to make life easier, and besides,
you'll find I'll rejoice right along with you if all goes really
smoothly and this turns out to be unnecessary."

Slowly I slid the raft of papers out of the folder to begin an hour long interview and examination. Conscious of how consuming the pile of papers could look to anyone whose energy was deficient, I joked, "Don't let these papers over-whelm you, Andy. I have more papers than brains. But I only have to fill out bits and pieces here. The rest I'll save for later, so it need not be too tiring." I glanced at him out of the corner of my eye. My corny joke had worked, and he visibly relaxed a little as he smiled.

"You'll find this a good chance to get acquainted as we go along. I'll have a much better feel for what you've been through by the time we finish, but do feel free to interrupt with anything you think is important. That's what it's all about." As efficiently as I could, I began the numerous checklists of information that summarizes, as factually as possible, that most personal of all struggles, the struggle to save a life. I wondered if the reason we deal with so many facts is it helps us keep our own emotions at a distance?

"After all, this is a life we're talking about here, a young life at that," I said to myself.

We established he was fifty-nine years old and had been ill for nine years. "Wow! Quite a track record," I rejoiced. "You've certainly learned to do something right to have conquered the challenges of all those years. Good for you!" I felt pride for him, and noted he suddenly looked taller, as he shifted in his chair and reflected on the many battles he had endured.

We talked with ever-increasing ease as he swung through the familiar terrain of what he had experienced. His origi-nal cancer site in the lymph nodes in his abdomen had been seemingly handled successfully, and he had returned to work with a sense of rejoicing, to once again ride the rails of

America. But he discovered a year later a spot had developed elsewhere. Thus began the multiple series of treatments, radiation, and chemotherapy to which he owed his life to date.

When it came time to fill in his medication schedule, he turned quickly to the three-drawer stand at his left and whipped out a well-worn folder. Large lined sheets of graph paper, stapled and taped together, were unfolded. Inside of four seconds flat, he was recounting every medicine, dosage, and time ingested of the many medications his physician had ordered.

"Very impressive," I said. "Mind if I just borrow that and write it all down? It's a real treat to see such organization and I must admit I don't get this treatment very often." He handed over the folder and leaned in my direction to be certain that I was going to fill in my form with the integrity of his.

Must be years of looking at train schedules, I thought. Wonder if this helps him feel more like he's still at work, keeping the schedule? It certainly helps me. Handing it back to him, I glanced up and listened intently as he further described the ins and outs of his routines. The schedule was a reflection of all the pieces of information about taking his medicines that only an alert patient, who carefully watches the signs and symptoms, can glean.

"You know, these two medicines don't mix right. Doesn't matter what the pharmacists say, these two must to be taken at least two hours apart. Never let anyone do it differently, nurse, because it just starts all kinds of problems," he instructed.

"Don't think I've ever heard that before. Tell me what you've discovered so I can pass it on to others and share the wealth." Andy then launched into an intensely lucid and helpful account of his experiences with his medications that his good detective work had discovered. How I admired his clear logic and obvious good thinking. "What wonderful things can be accomplished when patients continue to assume responsibility for their own well-being," I said.

Our interview went smoothly, as we slowly worked our way through the myriad of details that chronicled the specifics of his gallant fight. Then I slid into the physical assessment of Andy, who, by now, was relaxing as he warmed to recounting his struggle. I realized he had wonderful things to teach us all about the human spirit. "What a marvelous sense of pride he has to have come this far. This man surely has wonderful things to teach us about the indomitable human spirit," I said to myself.

Andy's cheerful easy conversation never flagged for an instance. All questions designed to discover just how much pain and suffering he was experiencing were deftly dodged as he reassured me he was feeling just great. The large doses of pain medicine told me otherwise, but I knew from years of experience patients long to be accepted where they are, not overridden by the cold clinical expertise of a professional. Being more knowledgeable than anyone else about his case, Andy presented me with a golden opportunity to discover more about him by listening, than I could know on my own.

An hour later, Andy had refused home health aide service, pastoral visitation, a medical social work consultation to make long range planning, and all my other suggestions, as he kept reassuring me he was "just fine." His examination said otherwise. By now the strain of bearing up and being just fine was taking its toll. I hastened to finish the interview, seeing no point in breaking down Andy's pride into an admission he was bluffing on this first encounter.

"I'll be back to check on you tomorrow afternoon, Andy, since your temperature is up a little bit. The medical world expects me to ride herd on these things, and although it is probably nothing, we'll both feel better when I see that for myself. Meanwhile, you are open to our services and should anything change, call the twenty-four hour phone number I've written down. Someone will help you right away."

I'll be in shock if he calls in and complains, I thought. Not his style. He's been so competent, he's so intelligent and such a good detective. My job is going to be to gain his confidence and let me be part of the team. "Wonder how long that will take me?" I asked myself.

Andy's cordial manner, as he bid me good-bye, set the tone for almost all our meetings to come. He remained cheerful, in control, and the picture of a man with no problems at all. Twice weekly visits continued for just under a month and then I got my first phone call.

"Hi, I'm in the hospital," Andy said, cheerfully. I had seen him the day before when he looked the very picture of health, and so I wondered aloud what had happened. "Just a little problem with a lung infection," he relayed, his voice raspy and altered by inhalation treatments.

How quickly he became ill! I thought. Startled and alarmed, I resolved to find some way to determine he had an infection much sooner in the future. Homecare is designed to prevent hospitalization by early detection of patient problems. Statistics have shown beyond doubt that early intervention achieves just that goal. I sure didn't catch that one, I thought. Well, you can't catch them all, Joy.

That set the tone for many months to come. He was well one moment, acutely ill the next. Gradually he relaxed with me, as I became more and more adept at reading the inscrutable Andy. Nurses become good at reading the unspoken signs. The angle of a head, the sudden slight shaking of the hands, subtle skin color changes, eyes that don't shine the same way, even the tone and pitch of voices are gentle clues something is different. It's as if we memorize what is usual for each patient, playing it against what we find that day. With Andy this became imperative.

After his second hospitalization, once again for sudden rampant infection, this time on a weekend, I sat down with Andy. "Listen. This is getting to be ridiculous. We have to talk turkey here. By now we've established you get sick easily. If you so much as sneeze, I want to hear about it! Can we cut a deal?"

Clearly I had begun winning him over to the point of view that I was on the team, and laughing, he responded with a promise to do that. "If that's what you really want, Joy."

He was as good as his word, and we began the many months of scrutiny that invariably improves the quality of life and established the smooth working relationship between patient and nurse.

If Andy phoned, I dropped everything as soon as possible and checked him out. This successfully kept him out of the hospital months at a time. Gradually, as his condition deteriorated he turned over more and more of the close scrutiny to me. But still no feelings came up in discussion. "I'm great; how are you?" remained the order of the day.

"It is unusual for a patient to hold onto his feelings and fears this tightly and for such a long time," I mused. On the one hand, I admired the determined Andy who lived each moment as fully as possible. On the other, I knew from experience that a patient who has not expressed his fears, concerns, hopes, and dreams is a ticking time bomb.

By now I was very familiar with his wife, who had to work to keep the family finances intact. Margie arranged to take vacation days at important times to be with Andy, and between those and the post-hospitalization conferences, we had established a solid and friendly relationship. She became a regular with her sister at the primary care giver support group I facilitated. We developed a close working relationship that included calls to her at work periodically to check what I was observing against her years of knowing Andy. The information we exchanged became invaluable in both directions. Still, no feelings surfaced from Andy.

Inspiration struck one day, when dogged by a series of emergencies and running behind schedule, I arrived at Andy's. I had eaten my lunch on the run in my car while driving, and held a freshly poured cup of tea from my Thermos in my hand. With a glimmer of invention I sat down and said, "Hope you'll forgive me if I just sit here and have my tea before we begin our visit, Andy." Our conversation turned to that of visitor and patient, and gradually I slipped into an easy tone. "Tell me what it used to feel like, Andy, when you discovered a fresh problem and had to face all the uncertain years. What was it like for you to discover you had cancer at age fifty?"

"That was the worst moment of my life! You can't imagine how bad it is, Joy. Margie and I cried and hugged each other and just clung to each other. There's been lots of bad moments but that was the worst."

"What was hardest about it?" Afraid to interrupt the pain he was releasing I coaxed him to tell me more.

"I didn't want to die. I just wanted to keep doing what I always did, riding the trains. I mean, I had to give that up when I was in Vietnam, and that was terrible. But I lived through it and got back on track only to find out now, I was probably going to die, and it wasn't fair!" The tears so gallantly held back welled up within Andy, and with a shudder, he began to cry. "I just want to ride the trains again. I never did anything to hurt anyone. Why do I have to go through this? It's not right! I've got too much living to do yet." His voice trailed off into a whisper, unable to override the emotion that finally carried him down the path so long avoided.

"It must have been awful, Andy. What got you through those times?"

"I don't know. I just made up my mind I didn't want to go yet. I decided there had to be a way to do this. And I did do it. I did! I'm sorry, Joy, this is terrible. I'm not supposed to cry."

"Andy, it's real. It's honest emotions. It doesn't mean anything except you're real. If you didn't feel that way, I would think we'd need to have your head examined. Tell me more about what it's been like for you."

The floodgates opened. "I licked it so many times only to have them find a new spot. Now they tell me it's all through my body. How am I going to do it any more? I don't know what to do. I'm tired! Tired of fighting. Tired of sitting in a chair. Tired of the pain. Tired of never being able to do what I want to do. When am I going to get back on my train?" By now his heaving shoulders said it all.

I strode to Andy's side, gently rubbing his upper back between the shoulders. "I know it's tough, Andy. But people don't change who they are. You've always done your best to fight and you'll find ways to keep doing that. Your strengths are there, and just like you have in the past, you'll take one day at a time.

"It will be okay to give up the fight whenever you're ready, Andy. Everyone will understand when you feel you can't fight any longer. Meanwhile we're here to help in any way we can. You know you can count on us to be here for you. Let's talk some about what could be ahead during my next visit. With some knowledge of what that could be, you'll find you won't feel quite as helpless."

He reached out from under the heavy emotion and took my hand. "I don't think I ever cried like that for anyone but Margie." Andy hung his head, carefully avoiding my eyes.

"Andy, you know I'm a straight-forward, call-a-spade-a-spade person. You have just honored me with the total truth as you know it. It's been awful for you! To be able to say how you feel is a sign of strength, not weakness. We have to deal with things as they really are. Otherwise we're all kidding each other and ourselves all the time. Not that we're going to have this conversation every day mind you. But right now you have trusted me enough to share the bitter truth, and I want you to know it increases my admiration for you." Slowly Andy regained his composure. And I had a burst of inspiration.

"What happened to the steam boilers if they weren't vented properly, Andy?"

"They blew," he replied. "High, wide, and handsome."

"Well, people are like steam boilers. If they aren't vented properly they blow, too. Part of my job is to drain off the pressure from you little by little, so what could be a disastrous explosion, becomes a small flare up." Andy was breathing slowly now, nodding slightly at my comments.

"You know, you're a pretty marvelous human being. Do you have any idea how many people you have inspired with your spirit? I, for one, will never forget you. Show me where it's written that you, and you alone, are the only one who must be perfect and never have a moment when the fight seems like too much."

Subtle shifts were beginning to ease the taut muscles in his shoulders and rigid back, shifts that told me my words were finding a place. "There is no such thing as perfection, Andy. In fact if we choose perfection we choose failure. There is no way to be the perfect patient, and to ask that of yourself is an act of cruelty." Andy raised his head to look at me. He looked startled.

"Perfection is an illusion," I went on. "What we do have, it seems to me, is the task to learn in this classroom we call life. Look at all you've learned, my friend. Did you know you were this strong, could be this tenacious when you started out?" Andy shook his head, still unable to talk, but clearly engaged.

"Did you realize how adaptable you could be to whatever came your way? Did you ever dream that life could mean so much, or you could see so clearly how precious it is that you could fight this hard?" His repeated head shaking gave me his answers in the only way he trusted himself to do.

"How about taking time for another act of honesty and add up the pluses of what you've learned? That won't take away the terrible moments, or all the fatigue you feel from fighting, but it will give you an honest overview of how much you have accomplished."

The sounds of sorrow had stopped. Now was the moment I knew Andy would be most embarrassed, when his eyes would meet mine again. I knew his humor, and I knew humor to be a great rescuer.

"Besides, Andy. I was beginning to think I was going to have to buy you this great t-shirt I saw. It has a cow on its back, feet up in the air, with the caption, "Really. I'm fine!""

The sobs turned to laughter and I hugged him. "Anyway, I saw it in Canada when I visited, and I haven't been able to figure out how I was going to get back there to buy one for you."

We fell into our usual pattern now as I resumed my role of community health nurse, executing the familiar routine of checking vital statistics and listening to his lungs.

"Next time I visit we'll share information and talk about some of the things we've been avoiding," I promised. "Then we'll get back to life as usual."

As I swung my car out of the drive, I reflected on what it had taken to reach Andy's real feelings. I said to myself, "How often people see not admitting their feelings as a sign they're doing fine, as if some prize goes to the one who can hold out the longest. What misunderstanding have we bought about the meaning of bravery to be able to pressure ourselves? Life is precious beyond description and to be facing the untimely loss of your life is cold and horrible. Can you see, Andy, saying so means opening the doors to finding new ways to deal with it all?"

I seriously doubted Andy saw it that way. I suspected that some embarrassment was mixed with the relief that he felt, at finally letting out the tidal wave of feelings he had held back for so long. I could only hope he would let the benefit of relief outweigh his embarrassment. As I drove to my next visit, I thought about cultures that allow men to cry, namely Irish men who cry at funerals.

I thought about what it would require to validate Andy to himself. I talked to myself, "All feelings are valid, even the urge to chuck it all. No feelings are automatically good or bad. Feelings are energy, and how we frame that energy in our thoughts is what shapes our emotions. Equally significant was how we frame our feelings by our intentions. If our intent is to get emotion out in front of us, where we can deal openly with it, then it is good, for there we can choose what else to do: cancel it, redirect it, savor it, or honor it. Do you see you are entitled to feel, Andy? That's speaking our truth. I sure have my work cut out for me on this one." I drove to my next client, but my thoughts were about Andy and his gallant struggle.

After that day, Andy went back to his usual demeanor of cheerful "Everything's fine" but we had completed our talk. For a brief moment he had learned it was safe to feel and that had opened the door for him. I told him of the possible ways his disease could develop, reassured him we would be able to deal with each one, and affirmed the medical system had many resources for dealing with any of the possibilities.

"There's even a hospice division we can enter, whenever that becomes the best option," I said.

"It'll be a long time before I need that, Joy. I'm fine!"

I wondered if Andy would be one of the patients who would never admit how sick he is and even die clinging to, "Really, I'm fine!" Man, he's tenacious! I thought.

Life proceeded with Andy calling me if he so much as sneezed, and I would check it out promptly and get right on the phone to the doctor and oncology clinic nurses. I sent him to the doctor many times and by so doing averted the disaster of another hospitalization. "At least we've come this far, Andy. You just keep telling me about the sneezes," I said.

Our agreement provided smooth sailing, with an occasional brief hospitalization for infection control thrown in. The hospital homecare coordinator and I would share information at such times. She was a buddy to Andy, seeing him very accurately and honoring that he had lived through the seemingly impossible more than once. "They should study you and see what they can learn," we told him when his blood counts plummeted to dangerous levels and then, two days later, kicked back in so he could return home.

We admired that indefinable something that kept him going, and longed to be able to bottle it and use it at will to help others. Was it genetics, determination, or pure gut level choice to keep fighting? "Probably some of all of that, but it would be great to know how to deliberately promote this in patients, if we only knew how," we kept saying to each other.

Margie continued her struggle. Nine years turned into ten, and she began to break down at support group meetings. "I don't know how much longer I can go on. I love Andy, but I've faced 'this is it' so many times, I can't feel anymore. It's like I've gone numb. They told me he had two years to live ten years ago. The children and I poured all the love we felt into Andy, and now we can't maintain the pace any longer. I had cancer myself a little over a year ago and my doctor keeps insisting I have to take care of me. When? Andy's needs get to be more, not less. The children are finding it hard to keep coming constantly and still raise their own children. What do you even tell children when it's gone on like this?"

"Margie, the amount of pain you are feeling is not an indication of your inadequacy," I gently suggested. "Rather, it's a measure of how much you love Andy. How much I wish I had known that when I experienced grief! In retrospect I saw I had really done well but at the time I felt so inadequate I assumed I was doing a terrible job. Right now I hear that in you, and I want you to know you have a choice to see it differently. You are doing a phenomenal job in a very rough situation. The fatigue, the pain, the feeling of not being able to take anymore...they are all measures of how much you have given and care."

One of the significant gifts of support groups is to validate the person's feelings while discovering truths that would otherwise become apparent many years later, out of the heart of the storm. The goal of support groups is to allow expression of feelings, but too many times I had witnessed someone going out into the night hurting, without the perspective that could lift the person to a new awareness of his strength. Now, we concentrated on Margie being able to see herself through our eyes. As the group sought to have Margie see her courage and how well she met the challenge, she began to relax.

"It's all right to be angry that this has gone on so long."

"How could anyone be expected to put forth such a gigantic effort for so many years? The real miracle of you is that somehow you have done a seemingly impossible job."

"We need to help you now realize it's all right to honor your own needs, find your own strengths, and carve out what you need for you." Margie looked up, and right before our eyes her posture grew an inch or so.

At my next visit, I was able to sell Andy on accepting a home health aide because of her needs. "Andy, Margie needs some time-out here. An aide can help you with your shower and personal care, and Margie can sleep an hour later each morning or go to bed an hour earlier. She can come home and have a cup of tea, instead of having to swing into action to get at the laundry, because you've been sweating out your fevers around the clock."

"All right. Anything for Margie," Andy capitulated quietly.

My call to the aid office to arrange services included a plea for someone skilled to be assigned, and I ticked off the reasons why this case was challenging. "We need to meet this patient where he is, giving him all the choices he can have, so accepting help doesn't chip away at his self respect. Please make it a really good one! This guy's a handful."

Kathy was a gift to anyone fortunate enough to receive her services. She was an experienced caregiver who had cared for her mother and a favorite aunt, both with cancer. "She is our best," I was assured.

From then on, we had a bigger team, and what a gift she was to Andy. If Kathy called to report a serious symptom, I got right over to Andy's house. With her superb command of the task before us and comprehension of just what Andy was feeling, we moved into an enviable position for helping Andy.

The magical Kathy managed to pry Andy out of the lounge chair, for at least a few hours each day, and into a hospital bed we set up in the living room for him. "To save your skin from wearing out," she had told him. Andy decided to listen to her. I had a cohort who got on the phone and clued me in promptly to the latest changes. Life ran smoothly once more.

Margie continued her progress. She began to think aloud in support group about the steps she might have to take if

Andy were hospitalized again and she didn't feel she could take him home. The guilt she felt over having to make a choice she feared would make Andy feel abandoned became an overwhelming emotion.

"What do we do with the guilty in our society?" I asked her.

"Punish them," she replied, after careful thought.

Nodding, I added, "You are setting up the potential for punishment, Margie, if you walk around with guilt. Feel guilty enough and sure enough, you'll find a way to punish yourself because you already believe guilty people need punishment. And guilt gives other people a handle by which they can manipulate us. Do you want that?"

"He does that already," she said, allowing herself to laugh. And I knew what she meant. Way too often I had seen care willingly given to a loved family member, only to find that unwittingly that set a pattern that evolved into a trap for patient and family alike. I have no trouble believing that's how it is with Andy, after so many years, I thought.

"As the years tick by, the best of intentions can turn into fatigue, while the patient's behavior evolves into games," we told her. I could only guess how much that intensified each year for Margie as the "only two years to live" had turned into ten.

Clearly we needed to help Margie find a new approach. "There is an expression I think you might like. 'What is just is. So deal with is-ness.' Something is not inherently good or bad, it just is. Now, Margie, you are free to say 'I have a very large case of is-ness here.'"

Margie tipped back her head and laughed. "A very large case of is-ness," she admitted. Fortunately, her sense of humor remained intact, and the laughter seemed to ease her pain.

"That's all that gets us through sometimes, Margie. Step back from the emotion a bit and look for the humor."

One day I arrived at my usual visit time. The gloom in the air was thick enough to slice up and serve. "He's thinking about dying," Kathy announced. "Wondering if it's soon."

Pausing to select my direction, I placed a hand on Andy's forehead, quickly reviewing his well-documented vital signs, checking lungs and blood pressure, reviewing the data at hand. Nothing was out of the ordinary. "Andy, I'd be rich and famous if I could predict when death could come for everyone. But to the best I can see, it's not going to be now. We do need to talk about it, though. I haven't sensed you wanted to do that, but you know, we must think about death now and then, even when we're well. It's a natural part of life, and not thinking about it doesn't make it go away."

Tears welled in Andy's eyes. I knew he couldn't talk so I carried the ball for a bit. "Who have you lost that you loved, Andy, and how did it happen?"

"My father." He sobbed. "He had a heart attack and it was quickly over. He was lucky."

"I don't know what philosophies you have about death, Andy. I know more than sixty people who have had near death experiences and who have remembered what dying was like. They tell me it is the most peaceful experience. Not only is it incredibly beautiful, but they could also see and hear, and knew what all the medical people and family attempting to revive them were thinking. Every one of them has reassured me that they are no longer afraid to die. In fact, they look forward to it. I can't help but conclude, Andy, that death is a beautiful spiritual experience that has received bad press."

His attention clearly gathered, Andy's sobs subsided. "In fact," I continued, "although I'm not ready to go any sooner than I must either, I have come full circle and look forward to the experience." His eyes glanced up and met mine with a mixture of what I read to be curiosity and amazement.

"The body is really the car you drive, Andy. You are the driver. When the vehicle breaks down the driver gets out and goes to find a vehicle that does work. In another place, one we can't see, but from which the driver can apparently see us. Maybe some day we'll be able to see them, too. A handful of people I have met do seem to see our loved ones around us."

"Really, Joy?"

"Just recently I had a family with seven adult children, several of whom could sense the presences in the room, and one of whom could see every detail and describe it all to us. It exactly matched what the patient was seeing. I'm hoping for a day when I can be one of those people, too." I waited for Andy's taut body to signal me he was willing to hear more. His shoulders were no longer hunched forward, and his facial expression was one of active curiosity peeking through the sadness.

"How do you feel about that, Andy? Does that make sense to you? Have you ever known someone with a near death experience?" I led the way for him to take the conversation in any direction he wished. "I don't say you have to see it like I do, Andy. I'm offering my observations so we can talk about what it is you do feel."

With his eyes turned to the side in concentration, he slowly replied. "You know, there was a guy I worked with who told me that. Seems he had an allergic reaction to one of the medicines he was given while in the hospital, and suddenly he found himself floating on the ceiling. The nurse ran out of the room calling for help. He just watched calmly as they all struggled to bring him back. He was calm. I remember him describing the peace he felt, and shaking his head that he could feel so peaceful while the whole room went nuts with nurses and doctors trying to help him. He said, 'Imagine. That was me down there and I was as unconcerned as could be. It's okay. I kept thinking. This is beautiful. Just let me be.'"

"And?" I inquired. Andy was on a roll and I didn't want him to stop now.

"When he told us all about it, I could hardly believe my ears. It was the strangest thing I'd ever heard. Kind of forgot about it, I guess. You mean, you've heard these things too, Joy?"

Nodding, I told him other stories of near death survivors. They had come from various sources, former patients, family members who were present with dying patients, even from doctors who had died and been revived. Books, personal meetings with some of the people who had been researched by Dr. Kenneth Ring and Dr. Raymond Moody, the pioneers, had rounded out my information. I had attended lectures given by some of these pioneering greats. I shared all this with the now curious Andy.

"I can echo this too, Andy," Kathy added. "I've taken care of patients who have had these same experiences, and I've been with many people when they die. You know I took care of my mother and aunt as well. It was beautiful and peaceful for them both, and they got beyond feeling fearful, even though they didn't think they would be able to do so."

The once-morose Andy was calm, his taut body now relaxing in his lounge chair. His troubled expression had given way to a soft smile of wonder. Eyes once so saddened were currently softly reflective. "It's amazing, Joy."

"In my desire not to avalanche you with constant talk about dying, Andy, I don't bring up this subject all the time. I realize you are very busy living and you are doing a great job of that. But I want you to know, anytime you do want to discuss what may be ahead, you can just say 'It's time to talk, Joy', and I'll know what you mean." I smiled tenderly at him, this tenacious and determined man, who had such capacity to endure.

"You know, it's really one of my favorite topics so don't feel any qualms about bringing it up." I laughed, but I recognized the truth I stated. The whole topic had always fascinated me.

We had succeeded in moving over some of his anxiety and making space for some new ideas. Andy was more mentally relaxed and at peace, but his body continued to deteriorate.

The oncology nurse at Andy's clinic apparently failed to believe me when I phoned in his latest emergency. I decided to visit the clinic and talk face to face about our efforts to help Andy.

"We see Andy in clinic one day, he's just fine, joking, problem-free and everything is wonderful. The next day you are calling and telling us he's in terrible shape. No one gets sick that quickly," she said.

"Andy does. I've even been at his house where he was fine without a trace of problems, only to have him become so ill a few hours later I had to hospitalize him." Then I added to myself angrily, "Haven't you heard of a compromised immune shield?" And then I checked myself, "Hold on, Joy. Arguing isn't going to help Andy."

"I've always appreciated how quickly you've responded to my requests. Andy is only alive now because we have worked out such a smooth team approach."

I knew this to be true. No one does it all alone. Teamwork made all the difference. However, the team included patient, aide, home care nurse, oncology staff, doctor, and family members. Not one of these was insignificant. Any professional who deludes himself into thinking he can see it all without accessing information from all of these is in a state of denial, I thought.

When I visited Andy, I said, "Listen, my friend. They think I'm nuts! How about knocking off this 'Really, I'm fine' routine and letting them in on how bad it gets for you. It's not too late to get the t-shirt with the cow on its back." Andy laughed hysterically at the image of his nurse, who fought for him, in hot water.

"It's just that I think everyone has problems, Joy, and I don't want to be the one to make it worse for anyone," he said quietly. I nodded, understanding the source of his response was genuine caring about others, and that concern cushioned my discomfort.

"That's because he saves it all and takes it out on us," Margie said in support group.

The group murmured their understanding of this syndrome and added their examples to the roster. "In one way, it's a positive that our loved ones feel free enough to say how they feel to us," I volunteered. "But taking it out on us still hurts. And doesn't feel fair. Why do you think they do this?"

"We're safe," said one. "They know we aren't going to go away."

"They count on us to know them well enough to know it isn't the way they always feel and that we will let go of the blame eventually," volunteered another.

"We're the ones at hand."

"Everyone has to be able to talk to someone or explode."

"How does that make you feel?" I asked as I looked around the group and noted the distraught faces.

"Awful!"

"Like I want to quit the job, resign, and let someone else take it for a while."

"Guilty. I mean, he's got it so much tougher than I have, how can I be so impatient with him? I can still get up and go out and everything. I really feel like an awful person at times." The answers came swiftly, the heart wrenching pain an unwelcome part of their experience. Tears of frustration welled in the eyes looking back to me.

"You have a right to your feelings, you know," I told them. "Being the brunt of someone's frustration isn't something anyone could ever learn to love. If you did, we would call it masochism. What do you do when this happens?"

"Sometimes I go into the bathroom and cry my eyes out," one responded.

"I go out to the garage and threaten to put my fist through the wall with my pounding," said a male. "Then I end up being hurt!"

"I feel guilty and like an awful person. Sometimes it lasts for a couple of days before I can pull out of feeling I have really let him down. I wonder who would ever want to take care of a rotten person like me, if I were in his shoes," said another.

Margie said, "I told God something had to give. And then I got cancer. So I said, 'Cancel that. It's not what I had in mind.' Now I just do my best to forget about it, but it still hurts."

"It does hurt. Yes, we are familiar and comfortable, and each of us lets off steam to someone we feel secure enough with and hope loves us enough to be able to take it. That's all true, and in a way, it's a demonstration of how they count on the love they receive from us." I paused to let that sink in.

"But, I think we could look at it another way. We are free to remind ourselves, 'This is the disease talking. He or she wouldn't talk that way without the horrible frustrations he's experiencing.'" Pausing, I saw the slowly nodding heads, as sadly they acknowledged the pain and frustration their loved ones were feeling.

"Having recognized that, we are free to say quietly, 'I know you are really angry at life and not at me, and I need you to know, while I'm angry at what has happened to you, I am also having trouble not feeling responsible for it. I feel if I could have done things better or differently, maybe this wouldn't be happening to you. My feeling inadequate isn't going to help anyone. Right now, I need to walk away, and we'll talk later when I won't pick up the blame.'"

Heads nodded again in agreement. "That takes practice to be able to say when the moment arrives. I suggest you say it aloud in the car going home, or at least your version of that point. Rehearse it as if you are to be in a play, so the line is ready on cue. It's necessary to honor your own truth and not feel you must be a giant among caretakers who can and must take everything that comes your way."

"Caretakers need to be helped to find solutions," I shared with them. "Wallowing in emotions without moving on to 'Now, what can I do about this?' leaves everyone mired in their self-pity. Experienced caretakers learn the pitfalls of feeling sorry for themselves. Left unchecked, self-pity is a one way street to feeling martyred. It's a trap. Unfortunately, knowing that doesn't stop the avalanche of feelings," I cautioned them.

"But what can we do when feeling sorry for ourselves happens?" The question was clearly on everyone's mind.

"Self pity is very real. You are entitled to feel that, and probably can't stop feeling it from time to time. It needs to be expressed honestly and acknowledged. Sit with it, feel it intensely, and then drop it, as a clear-cut conscious choice, so something else productive can move into the space."

Thoughtful expressions eased the faces that held anger only a moment ago. "Been there, done that," one offered, to nodding heads all around. Gradually pain eased from their taut bodies at the prospect of having a new tool to use, and they sat back into their chairs as they allowed themselves to realize that what felt so objectionable to each of them was shared experience "normal" to caregivers.

"And if we don't drop it?" asked Margie.

I went on. "The alternative is a rapid spiral into feeling sorry for oneself, which eventually robs our power and traps us. Add that to your fatigue from long stretches without enough sleep, worry about the future, your torn feelings of inadequacy, and it spells disaster for you as caregivers."

The calm voice of Paul, my volunteer assistant, was soothing as he added his perspective to the group. "The one you love knows you really care, or you wouldn't still be there doing what you are doing."

It was as if a gentle breeze swept through the room and cleared away the lackluster air. We felt the group move out of their intense emotions and into the calm of understanding and into acceptance of the importance of what they provided by their ongoing love and caring.

"Doing and saying nothing does leave me feeling power-less," said one.

"To know a way to handle things that gives me my self respect when the moment happens feels good. Like it could give me a feeling of having some power back," said another.

"This must be one of the most un-talked about factors we are facing. Cancer, or whatever terminal illness we have, robs us of our power." Margie added.

On the wave of our shifted mood, we ended the evening with hope once more. Within each of us was the possibility for many responses. Shifting our pain was paramount to reaching a better way.

Margie's take on this the next day confirmed the shift. "I feel a lot better. Not so guilty about what I've been thinking."

"All that is ever available for us in every experience is the ultimate thought we choose to think," I told her. "That is all the power we truly have in each moment. Congratulations on taking back your power."

"I guess the final choice of how I am going to feel about Andy's outbursts is mine," Margie said, thoughtfully. "Now if I can only remember that."

"You'll be able to do that, Margie. As a nurse, watching the wonderful people I meet, I see the power clear choice initiates. Others have taught me choosing holds enough power to shift our response into something we wish to think, not something we find there from old habit or from feeling so pushed and inadequate."

"Thanks, Joy," she said.

"You're very welcome, Margie. I'm thankful for the incredible lessons from the patients and families I've known, including you."

Remembering all those patients and their families, I paused now to look out the train window at the terrain, the beautiful seacoast beginning its stretch to the sea. Light streamed onto the glistening water, and surfers were running happily from sandy white beaches into the swelling waves. "You would have loved this train, Andy. Maybe this is one of the routes you took. I'm riding the train and remembering you," I said to myself.

Kathy had clued me into the fact that Andy was missing the children who were visiting infrequently. Privately Margie added her understanding of the situation. "They just don't know what more to do or say. It's gone on for so long, everyone has run out of ways to be helpful."

"I know. Yet, we are setting them up for guilt of their own if we don't try to work this out. Do you think they would agree to a family conference where we can talk with Andy about what is happening, so he'll understand and they won't hate themselves when he dies?"

"I'll ask them," Margie said.

Andy's daughters all readily agreed to meet early one evening, when baby-sitters could be arranged. That took a couple of weeks to accomplish, when schedules could be coordinated. I agreed to be present. It didn't take us long to see the emotional conflict everyone was feeling. Nevertheless all were willingly present and now courageously working to heal the pain of seeing their father so ill for such a long time.

Andy sat on the edge of his bed, love for his family shining unmistakably from his face as he savored the moment. His beaming smile settled on each one, his gaze happily sweeping the circle of loved ones, proud to show off his family to his nurse.

Gently we inched into the process of getting comfortable talking about this most uncomfortable topic. We started the slow dance by becoming acquainted with happy stories about their children interlaced with memories of their own childhood days. Familiar family jokes were playfully revisited and enjoyed as if new. The comfort of the past paved the way. From that place of peace we tackled the more painful stories of Andy's prolonged battle.

"Tell me what it feels like to be in your shoes," I encouraged his children.

"I feel so inadequate. I want to help, but I just don't know what to do."

"I don't even know what to say anymore. Feels like I've said it all until I'm a broken record."

"The hardest thing is the pain. Dad tries to cover it, but I know him so well, and I just can't stand to see what the pain does."

Understanding dawned on Andy's face and I gently nudged him. "Seems like maybe they could feel guilty, Andy. What do you think about that?"

"I don't ever want any of you to look back and feel guilty!" Andy exploded. "No sir! You have all been there for me, and I can understand just how hard that has been for you. It's tough for me, too. But the important thing is that you remember how much you've done for all these years!"

"We'll do that, Dad, if you'll understand how much we love you and are going to miss you. We're already missing you at the thought of what's ahead," said his oldest.

Moistened eyes met as they connected with each other, united in understanding of their shared pain. As they voiced aloud the feelings held within for so long, the family pulled back together with a fresh perspective and melted into a loving group hug. They all said, "I love you," and the mood eased as each accepted the truth of the moment; they were grappling with an incredibly difficult challenge. There really aren't any maps made, no scripts written for how to do this year after year, I thought. It's a wonder anyone finds his or her way.

Not long after this meeting Andy took another trip to the hospital. This one was extremely serious, and I received a call from the homecare coordinator on duty at the hospital. "Doesn't look like he'll make it this time. Looks like we're running out of luck."

"I'll do my best to get over there before it's too late. If this is really it, I need to say my own goodbye." By the time I visited him two days later, the indomitable Andy had bounced back from the precipice one more time, greeting me as ever with a cheery appraisal this was just life as usual. "This is amazing. I half expect him to say, 'I'm fine, really!'" I marveled to myself. There was one important difference. Confusion had set in. Hard as it was to understand, hospital personnel concluded it was Margie and I who were confused. Andy's incredible ability to hone in and focus on the moment, putting everything he had into being normal in conversation, was nothing short of remarkable. It was a very convincing act that continued to work in the hospital setting.

The floor doctor decided to check out Andy's confusion for himself. "Who's the president of the United States, Andy?" he inquired.

"Oh, you know that bozo..."

"Yeah, you're right, Andy. George is a bozo."

"Yeah, George really let us all down, didn't he?" Andy added casually.

"You see," said the doctor to our homecare coordinator, "He's not confused."

"Doctor, he's not the only bozo we've had for president and besides, you filled in the name."

It had begun to occur to us that Andy was so much a part of all our lives that his team was also having problems accepting he would eventually die.

At our next support group meeting, an angry Margie said, "After all the years I've taken care of him and done everything they have ever asked, and they treat me like that! You'd think I had the mental problem."

"Did it ever occur to you that the doctors are having trouble letting go of Andy? After all, he's pretty remarkable and it sounds like they're losing a friend." Paul's quiet voice interjected. "How many years has it been they've been able to help him? Ten? Now it's eleven? It must be awfully hard to know your best efforts for eleven years are not going to make it in the final moment."

"Wow! I never thought of that. I guess if it's hard for me, I can understand it's hard for them, too," Margie reflected.

"I can vouch for how hard medical people take it when the long successes and special people just aren't going to make it after all," Paul said.

"Margie, even though that's true, how is it feeling for you at this moment? It's still valid for you to think anything you are thinking, and we need to honor your feelings," I said.

"I feel trapped. I have to go to work. I even want to go to work because I'd go out of my mind having to sit and watch him in all that pain all day, every day. But I don't know when I'll come home and find him dead on the floor. And I keep getting up at night to check on him. The doctor isn't dealing with the screwed up checkbook, or finding the things Andy loses. He isn't having the conversations that don't make any sense, all the while Andy insists his point of view is right."

"Tell us how you are doing this," the group pleaded. Like a shaken bottle of soda with its cap removed, Margie's frustrations rushed out, until the choked up place of discontent gave way to a quiet sigh.

Slowly we were able to persuade her what a phenomenal job she was doing. As she began to feel more successful and less inadequate with our reassurances, we were able to address another painful subject.

"Margie, how are you preparing yourself for a time when you might find Andy dead when you get home from work one day? How would you handle that?"

There was no gentle way to ask.

"I think I just accept that some things are out of my hands," she replied, quietly. "I mean, through the years there have been so many possible moments when he almost died. No one could say why he lived. If the medical people can't figure it out, why should I pick up the blame? I'm doing the best I know how to do every day. I guess I just have to accept what is just is, and what will be just will be." The tightness in Margie's face had given way to a look of sad but peaceful acceptance as she allowed herself to add up what the years had taught her. Paul and I exchanged glances and thought the philosophy had a familiar ring.

"Hooray!" the group exploded.

"Good going!"

"Congratulations!"

"Let's talk about what any one of us can do if we ever find someone in our care has suddenly died," I said. Carefully, step-by-step, we walked our group through the possible ways for getting immediate help, reinforcing the wonderful attitude of acceptance Margie had summarized. Equipped with knowledge, they felt at least a limited amount of confidence within their grasp.

Margie was able to bring Andy home one more time. Armed with a new awareness of her strength, she found ways to deal with the confusion that was now part of the picture. Not all days were equal. But on good days Andy still found life fulfilling.

In support group we challenged Margie to think about what she would do in life, once Andy died. "I don't know. He's been dying for so long, I've never thought about that," she said.

"How about you make a list of things you are looking forward to doing, and come up with a plan? Think about how you'll fill the time and handle the rough moments when they happen. Figure out your first priority. Then next meeting, tell us what you think, and we'll talk about that important adjustment period," I urged.

Margie did just that, and two weeks later when she talked about her plans for spending time with her grandchildren, baking cookies, and taking small overnight trips, we knew she had begun plans that would help her reinvest in the future.

Meanwhile, Andy found another burst of strength. The local Memorial Day parade was just around the corner and he was determined to go. A Vietnam veteran, he donned his uniform and managed to be in his electric wheelchair at the reviewing stand, as he had for so many years. The picture that captured his pride and salute for the newspaper also showed Margie in the background, in support of Andy, as she was every day of his life.

A thoughtful friend photocopied a hundred prints for him and Andy began to give them to special people. "Can I have one for my office, Andy?" I asked.

"I've already inscribed one for you, Joy," Andy said. On the picture were the words, "To the best nurse anyone could ever have, Love, Andy." Tears filled my eyes as I accepted the touching tribute.

"I still have that picture on my office wall," I said to Andy through my spirit. "You see, Andy? I do think about you all the time like I said I would." The train rode on, and I went on remembering.

Having made it successfully through the parade, it became clear Andy's strength was running out. "How much longer will it be, Joy?" he asked.

"I don't know, Andy. One thing we all have to recognize, though. The soul's in charge and it does know what it's doing. The rest of us attempt to participate in a meaningful fashion. Your soul has brought you this far. We can trust it the rest of the journey. After all, it's done a better job up to now then we ever could have, so you're in good hands."

When the moment came it was sudden. No great big marker stood out that this was to be the day. Andy awoke and was very restless. Margie didn't leave for work on time, and when Kathy came to do his personal care, she said, "I think we'd better call the nurse." As chance would have it I was on a day off and couldn't be reached, but another nurse came in my place. Margie remained calm, Andy got his wish to be at home when he died, and after his medicines were adjusted he eased into a peaceful half sleep. "He just looked calm and accepting," Margie said later. She was at his side in death as she had been in life.

Margie found she had learned what she needed to know and was able to accept that when death came; it was out of her hands to do any more. Andy took one last slow breath, and Margie caught the peaceful smile on his face that could be seen, if those around one dying catch just the right moment.

I looked out the window at the coast, the sun a ribbon of shining light creating a path across the ocean. The tide surged forward, its fingers of icy water lapping at the feet of laughing swimmers flirting with the tide, and I noticed a new moon in the sky. There is a time and a season for everything under the sun, I thought. "Symbols are everywhere, Andy, that life goes on in a new dimension. Are you driving a train where you are? I'm riding one down here thinking of you."

As I stepped off at the station of my final stop, I stood back and watched the train preparing to pull out. "All aboard!" I heard the familiar words, and without a backward glance, I picked up my suitcase and walked away from the platform to my new destination.

Anchor

Life is not marked by the number of breaths we take, but by the moments that take our breath away.

~ Anonymous

"They screwed up my medications, Joy. Every freaking time I go to the hospital they change all my medications around and mix them up. Now I'm having all sorts of problems I didn't have before I went in there. No one ever listens to me!" The explosive words had come out of the blue, in an otherwise non-committal conversation that offered no clues to his frustration. I was startled to see he had tears forming in his eyes.

I said to myself, "Not this again! Why don't medical people listen to patients? I have learned so much about medications by hearing what they say."

"Jack, I am someone who listens to patients. I've learned a great deal about what I know from doing that. Who wouldn't listen to you?"

"Some young kid, fresh out of school or something. She didn't have any experience or anything." His lean and tanned face was drawn into a tight frown that mirrored his frustration.

I had a perfect picture of what had happened. "Well, Jack, I've been around long enough to know how much less I know than I once thought. One of my favorite doctors used to say he knew more when he graduated from medical school than he ever has since. Now he realizes each year how much he has to learn." Jack laughed, in spite of himself, at the thought anyone could admit that, and his serious, angry expression gave way to an amused half-smile.

"Why don't you tell me what you used to do, and I'll see if we can resurrect the schedule."

Jack did indeed have a "screwed up" schedule, and in his weakened state, with side effects from strong drugs and the ravages of his illness, he was fighting desperately to regain some measure of control. Together we began the painstaking task of trying to sort out what worked with his twenty-six medications, many of which he knew didn't mix in his system at the same time. It took over an hour to sort out all the problems. By then, I could clearly see side effects were clouding his thinking, and his once straight posture had given way to a tired slump.

"Look, I'll come back tomorrow with a chart and we'll set this up together. We'll pour your medications into a pill box for a whole week. Then you'll be able to sit back and give it a little rest. Okay with you?" He accepted my offer. "This way, if you have to go back into the hospital again we'll have a correct schedule you can take with you. Maybe that will help."

"I'm never going back to a hospital again!" I let the remark pass unanswered, as I knew he was verbalizing how every desperately ill patient feels who wants only to have every precious moment safe in his home with family about

him. I doubted we could deliver on his desire to never go
to the hospital again.

My relationship with Jack began that day. Little did I
think, then, that it would be such a wonderful blessing.
Linda, his attractive, friendly sister, had met me at the door
and said in hushed tones, "Before you meet my brother, I
want to warn you he's had some bad experiences with
medical people. So, he doesn't trust anyone easily. I don't
know how much time you have, but if you can, stay a little
and talk with him. He usually warms up quickly to people.
It's just, right now he's not too open." Her large brown
eyes studied me, assessing my response to her request, wondering if I would be open to her help in meeting her
brother's needs.

"Actually, I allow a fair amount of time to meet a new
patient. But thanks for the advance information. That
helps." I glanced at my admission sheet and noticed Jack had
been in and out of hospitals.

"That's enough to rattle anyone," I mused to myself.
"Nothing to make you feel like you're losing control over
your life like repeated emergencies that tear you out of your
home!"

Linda had ushered me into a room off the kitchen, a
delightfully sunny square room with large windows over-
looking a beautifully landscaped pool. There was a sign,
"Enjoy life. This is not a dress rehearsal", and under it sat
Jack, a slender, reserved man, who regarded me soberly. Even
if the paper work in front of me didn't confirm it, I would
have known this young man had AIDS. His thin, chronical-
ly ill look told me he had been through a rough time, and I
didn't doubt for a second the hospital held bad memories
for him.

I accepted a cup of coffee and sat down on the comfort-able overstuffed couch, deciding to follow Linda's advice. "Before we do all the technical stuff called paperwork, tell me about yourself," I began. Slowly I set about winning the confidence of a very ill man who had seen more hospitaliza-tions, by half, than anyone ought experience. I wondered how long it would take me to gain the trust of someone so weary from his struggle. The polite, but reserved conversation seemed to be going nowhere, until Jack's sudden explosive outburst over his medicines told me so much. I told myself, "Did you ever get lucky, Joy. Whatever key unlocked that pain just saved you weeks of getting to know each other." Jack's confidence in me began that day.

After that, there were good days when things went well and Jack could feel in control. I visited him every week in the comfortable colonial house that he now called home. The coffeepot was always warm and ready to take away the chill of the autumn air. The problem was there were fewer and fewer good days. On the bad days, when he was acute-ly ill, Linda and I would confer in the kitchen or outside on the step as I arrived, safely out of earshot. "I just can't stand to see him so ill," she cried. I held her and comforted her, and then she dried her eyes saying, "I can't let him see I'm crying."

Pulling herself together, she returned to the perky and carefree manner she could exude so well and entered Jack's room with a little joke. It was a performance worthy of an Academy Award and my admiration for Linda grew to enor-mous proportions, as I watched her bring as much joy and confidence as possible into a life she recognized was per-ilously close to being over. "He's my brother," she would say, her determined chin held high.

Helping Jack was a whole family project, with Linda's teenage daughter, Michelle, bouncing in from school to sit and talk with Uncle Jack. Perching on the edge of the couch, she shared her day with Jack, and her brown eyes would twinkle as she made him laugh. On not-so-good days, her sensitive and caring face let Jack know she understood and was there for him. She was a treasure, and Uncle Jack was incredibly proud of her, with good reason. Linda's husband often had difficulty sleeping, as did Jack, and the two of them spent hours talking or watching a movie. He had added the large sunny room to the house when Jack came to live with them. When I had the opportunity to admire that, he said simply, "Hey! He's family!"

Even the dog, Coco, was part of the family support team. Devoted to Jack, the curly black poodle was never far away. Most often he curled up on the bed, near enough to keep tabs on Jack and check out the visitors in case Jack needed his protection.

"I hope Coco isn't in your way, Joy. He doesn't like to leave me alone," Jack said.

"Animals tell me a great deal about how the people are doing. If someone is in pain, the pet seldom leaves his side. Animals frequently know someone is very ill before medical people do. Then the pet sits guard, preferably on the bed and won't leave. Believe me, when Coco starts to do that I'm going to pay attention," I explained.

"Never thought about it like that! Coco, I have new respect for how you are looking out for me," Jack said. He reached over and scratched Coco affectionately under his chin.

The bond between patient and dog reminded me of the many faithful pets I had witnessed. When it became time for their charge to die, pets usually would not leave the patient untended. They would even skip eating and drinking to keep their faithful watch. However, when a patient was near death and the pet was casually walking around the house, I knew I could relax a little. Obviously the pet was comfortable enough to relax his guard for a few minutes. At the time of death, the animal usually withdrew and sat facing the patient's bed in solemn watch, as if to be out of the way, to let the person do what he must. I had learned to accept clues from the household pets. "Wonder if Coco will be my early warning signal for Jack?" I asked myself.

Even though Coco seldom left Jack's side, Coco was Linda's dog, and Linda was God's gift as a primary care giver.

She could spot a problem, and most of the time, she had the problem figured out by the time I arrived. I will never forget her logic and resourcefulness. Frequent emergencies happened without warning. Linda would skip outside and give me the details, and let off steam, all laughter gone from her chocolate eyes that seemed a family trademark.

One day she met me with, "He just had the strangest reaction right after he took that new evening medication last night. His eyes kind of rolled back into his head, and he got all funny and didn't make any sense when I talked to him. It was scary! It just wasn't my brother. I couldn't get in touch with the doctor, so I told him to stop taking the drug until the doctor called back. It felt like he was having a drug reaction to me." Linda's hands remained calm, but her face was drawn and tight with all the responsibility. "Fortunately, when the doctor called back, he said he agreed with me."

"You are a wonderful example of the phrase 'just do it, you can shake later,'" I said. I realized I could rely on her judgment. Whenever she called it was always important, and I learned I'd better get right over there when the message was from Linda.   One of Jack's doctors was particularly responsive to our concerns. Whenever I needed help I would call him. Thus, we established tight teamwork that mostly kept Jack out of the hospital and helped Linda feel more secure.

Linda, who loved decorating for the holidays, started early to decorate the house for Halloween. Her collections of memorabilia for each major holiday of the year had been accumulated over a long time. She and Jack had frequented craft sales for years, before he became too ill. Jack would happily spend hours helping her decorate. Now she pushed him on less well days to do so, knowing it could lift his spirits. Soon the house was filled with ghosts and goblins, and toothless pumpkins smiled their irresistible grins from cobwebbed perches.

On one visit, I walked into the kitchen and ducked under the curtain of cobwebs that stretched across the doorway, straight into the path of a toothless witch flying across the kitchen on a broomstick. Preparing to enter Jack's cheery room, a scarecrow jumped out at me and suddenly the jeering sounds of the Wicked Witch of the West, laughing raucously, were added to the background sounds of creaking gates and long sinister groans. Laughing, I stopped at Jack's bed and said, "This is great! I usually fly solo as the only witch around, Jack."

"You'd better be prepared to enjoy Halloween, Joy. It's Linda's favorite holiday." Coco kept his watch on the bed underneath the larger-than-life black spider that now graced the wall, unfazed by the sinister threat just above his head.

From then on each visit was an adventure. "Lift that box cover over there, Joy," Jack would urge.

"This is a set-up." I laughed, but tenuously did as asked. "Why do I have the feeling this box is rigged?" Out popped a ghost, moaning softly, and a bat suddenly whizzed by my head. Jack's shaking shoulders and hearty laugh told me it was worth taking the chance.

Decorating was only one creative way Linda made Jack's life richer. She had an uncanny knack for knowing exactly what was on his mind. One way or another she would clue me into the pressing issue, and together we would search for ways to assist Jack in handling the newest heartache or worry.

"He's not saying much, and I figured something was eating at him. On a hunch, from the upstairs phone where he couldn't hear me, I called the hospital clinic he visited. One of the guys he knew really well just died. I know he doesn't want to tell me because he thinks it makes me worry. Maybe you can just accidentally stumble onto this. I know he needs to talk to someone to feel better, and I guess it can't be me. Don't let him know I told you."

Not that we could fix everything that happened to him, but this was important enough we needed to try. Her insightful presence was a gift to Jack beyond any perspective I could have hoped to achieve.

"Bad day, Jack?" I asked. His silent nod confirmed the message from his somber face. "Want to talk about it?" I asked, as gently as I could.

"I don't want to worry Linda, but one of the guys I know from clinic died, and I feel pretty bad. He fought awfully hard. It doesn't seem right he didn't make it." He stared at the floor, a look of utter dejection on his face.

"That's tough! How does it make you feel to hear about this?"

"Helpless. Pretty helpless." Jack looked up now and met my gaze. "I've lost a lot of friends I've come to know at the clinic. It never gets any easier, Joy. Never any easier."

"What do you do to handle it, Jack? Do you allow yourself to express the pain, even cry?"

"Mostly I sit with it and try to work it through by myself, so I don't make it harder for those around me. I know it makes it bad for Linda, thinking about the time ahead." He paused, and I felt his tender regard for Linda. "Sometimes I cry, but I try to wait until she's gone to bed. It's about the only thing I can really do for her, try to make it easier."

"You can always talk to me, Jack. Just signal me with, 'I need to talk,' and I'll come as soon as I can." As I pulled up a chair he broke into a tiny smile, his expression full of gratitude, but his dull and lifeless eyes held the pain. He vented his sadness a bit, until I saw a more hopeful expression on his face and I knew he had let me comfort him. Gradually we moved on to other topics.

At other times of crises he would say, "I can't deal with it now, Joy. I just can't do it."

"I will honor that, Jack. Whenever you're ready, I am. Just signal me."

Little by little he let down his guard and tentatively he let me see the Jack underneath the bravado, a very tender, caring man who worked at living as fully as his ravaged body would permit. He learned I was there for him and we began to talk about what mattered most to him: living as well as possible in the remaining time he had. The real Jack had severe pain every day, but he didn't complain in an effort to keep going. He was afraid and did not want to die, but he fought bravely to conceal his fears from the loving family around him, especially Linda. When Jack began to see me as more than a nurse, we became friends.

One day Linda called, her voice quivering, "My brother's losing his eye sight, I just know it."

"I'll be right there, as fast as I can and be safe." I said.

Outside the kitchen door where she greeted me, I asked, "What makes you certain, Linda?"

"When we decorated for Halloween, I couldn't find one box of his favorite decorations. Then I remembered where they were. When I hung some of them, he never even noticed. I've been suspicious he was having trouble, so I kind of tested it again by hanging his favorite ghost over his bed. He still didn't see it. Joy, I don't think I can stand it! What will he have left if he can't see?" She sobbed.

"He'll still have you, Linda," I tried to reassure her, as I wrapped my arms around her and held her until the heart-breaking sobs ceased. "We need to wait and see what the doctor finds before we decide what we're facing. I promise you I'll get right on this."

"Just don't tell him I told you. He has so much pride!" Linda wiped away the tears, struggling to erase all the signs of panic from her face and find an expression that offered no clues to the unsuspecting Jack. Taking a deep breath and resetting her determined shoulders, she entered the house.

Inside I behaved as usual while going through our now familiar routine, waiting for an opportunity to test his sight. Eventually I handed Jack a bottle of medication. "Would you open that for me?" I asked. "Oh, which one did I hand you?" Out of the corner of my eye I saw him squint and then try to cover the fact he couldn't read the label. "Jack," I said, taking his hand gently. "Are you having trouble reading that?

For a long, suspended moment he held my gaze. "I've been trying not to notice." His voice was barely more than a whisper.

In silence we held hands for a moment each understanding the significance of what had just been said. "How long, Jack?"

"For a while. I didn't say anything. I've been around this disease long enough to know what it means, Joy. I can't imagine how I'll deal with blindness on top of everything else."

"Thanks for being honest with me, Jack. I know this is one of the toughest moments for you." Slowly he looked up and met my gaze. "Can I say I've been around long enough to see that we need to wait and see what the doctor says before we decide too many things?" His silence told me how he felt and I went on.

"The treatments available now are much different than we've had for many of the years you've been watching the scene. There may well be something we can do. It's so important to hold those positive thoughts you are so good at thinking."

Jack nodded. "I know you're right, Joy. I'll do my best. But this is the pits!" His voice quivered as he gamely fought back tears.

I went to the phone, as he surely knew I would, and made an appointment to have his eyesight checked on an emergency basis.

His test results confirmed what Linda had guessed. "I'm decorating the house right now for Christmas while he can still see," she said. "It's his favorite holiday and he's not going to miss it!" I gave her arm a squeeze. Blindness was one of the most threatening conditions that could happen in AIDS patients and she was refusing to give in to the panic.

Two days later I arrived to find the house decorated simultaneously for Halloween and Christmas, and Linda had mobilized her mother and sister to make Christmas cookies. The kitchen was decorated with bells and angels, hung between the patches of cobwebs and cornstalks. A large ceramic tree, decorated with ornaments blinked its cheery invitation to enter Jack's room, which now had a large angel hung over the bed where the massive spider once hung. A musical Santa Claus spun round and round on top of the television set, playing a succession of carols. I took Linda aside, hugged her, and said, "You're the best. How do you do it?"

"I'm willing to be the anchor," she said. "If he's going to go blind, then he's going to have seen Christmas first. I'll make every day from now until then Christmas if that's the only way I can have my brother see it." For a few days, her fierce protection of Jack held back the pain we would have to endure if he did lose his eyesight.

In front of Jack I carried on the festive spirit. "Boy, I don't know which one of us is losing it, but I could swear I see two holidays out there. Do you realize you'll be inundated with trick-or-treaters when the word gets around? They'll all be saying, 'Don't miss that house,' and expecting to get a Christmas present."

"Where have you been, Joy? This is the way everyone does it. What kind of sheltered life do you lead?" Jack asked. He told me stories about collecting the memorabilia all around the room, his expression rich with delight, as Christmas lights faithfully blinked in time to the music.

The new medication for his eyesight meant Jack would have to have very potent drugs administered through a circulatory port in his chest. It was a desperate attempt to halt the disease for him and Jack needed to be prepared. "I'm not going back to the hospital, Joy. I'm not!" He had clearly dug in his heels. "If I'm going to die I want to do it right here. I don't want to die, Joy. It's too soon. But don't take me out of here." He began to cry softly, shoulders heaving as he fought to stifle the tears.

"Jack, I don't say I blame you," I said. "But I really don't think you are dying right now. If I can talk the doctors into you receiving the bulk of your intravenous medicines here on home care, will you go in long enough to get them started? Linda's so good we can teach her how to manage, and you'd qualify for some extra help on a part-time basis. How about it, Jack? You know Linda will be brokenhearted if you can't see Christmas with her, and this has a really good chance of helping." I was making a desperate bid for compromise, counting on the thought of a brokenhearted Linda softening his resolve.

"Anything for Linda," he said. "Don't tell her I said so, Joy, but I know this is a lot harder on her than she lets on. She thinks she's fooling me and so I play along with it, but I know she's hurting a lot more than she admits." I squeezed his hand, tears misting my eyes. How touching it was, when someone loved another enough to endure the thing he most dreaded to help the other.

"What a gift they give each other! It's loving beyond oneself I'm watching and it's beautiful," I said to myself.

He returned from the hospital after three days, his medication schedules once more a mess. For a time I made daily visits to teach and supervise the new procedures. To put Linda more at ease I would sit in the comfortable chair and chat with Jack, while she, jaw set in fierce determination, overrode her feeling of insecurity and did the finest job of learning complicated treatments I have ever seen a stressed caretaker do. "Linda, don't plan on retiring," I told her. "You have to be here for me when it's my turn. I am going to pitch a fit unless you're the one who looks after me." Jack's anchor looked pleased.

The medications worked and the eyesight loss halted temporarily. The patient saw another "miracle to hold back the hands of time," as Linda and I called them. Jack began to make plans aloud to go to California where a specialist had found a new treatment for just such cases.

It was the talk of California that did it. Sitting and talking about his plan one day I asked, "Ever been to California, Jack?" The flash of darkness that crossed his face surprised me. There was a long pause while I waited.

"That's where this started. I was a foolish kid just out of high school and I couldn't wait to see the country."

"You went to California. Tell me about it."

"I went almost as soon as the ink on my high school diploma was dry. I loved it there. It was just at the height of some pretty wild times and I didn't even know about HIV. Hell, if I had, I wouldn't have listened. Who can tell a young kid like that anything, let alone about danger? By the time I was twenty-six I found out I had HIV and although I never said anything to anyone, I decided right then and there that was it. I wasn't dating any more because there wasn't any way I was ever giving someone else this disease." He looked at me to assess my reaction. Quietly he added, "And I never have, Joy. Not even once."

"Did you come right back east?"

"Hell, no. I had a few more years there feeling pretty good and not feeling sick. As long as I could, I stayed where I loved being."

"And how did you fill the years, Jack?"

"To tell you the truth, Joy, I don't usually talk about this. Linda knows all of this, but I don't tell others. I decided I needed to do something I could be proud of with my life. I needed to help someone else before I couldn't do it. There was a young woman from China who had struggled and saved and managed to get a visa to work here. It had been her dream to save enough money to immigrate to the U.S. with her three small children so her kids could have a chance in life. We worked at the same place, so I knew her story and I really admired her." He paused, eyes far away remembering.

I waited, wondering what he would reveal of his life to me that was usually kept in the private reaches and seldom shared. "She was a good person who had experienced a really tough life. She had guts and worked unusually hard, but she just couldn't swing it. She was set to go back in two weeks time and she was devastated. Her dream was dead.

"So I said to her, why don't we get married? It would be a marriage in name only, because I wouldn't take any chances on giving anyone my illness. Besides, we weren't in love. But I figured I had suddenly found out how precious life can be. How could I ever feel good again if I didn't give the gift of life to her and her children? So, we were married. I helped her bring the children to the U.S and they're doing fine in California."

"Does she know how it is for you now, Jack?"

"No, not really. We're still married, technically. She would do anything for me she could. I don't see letting her know how bad it is now, Joy. She would only feel she couldn't do for me what I did for her. That's not the point anyway. I did it to help others who couldn't get the help any other way. I did it so my life achieved at least one thing I could be proud of. I didn't want to die wondering if I ever made a difference to anyone."

"You make a difference, my friend, to a lot of people. One of them is your nurse." I couldn't say more and keep my composure.

Soon Coco began to spend more and more time on the bed and I knew I had to talk with Jack about the time ahead. We stayed so upbeat in between handling emergencies, I wondered how to broach the subject of death and dying. Generally a patient leads the way by saying something that naturally leads into the subject. Hospice nurses learn to watch all the nuances of everything their patients say and do, for clues as to where they are with their emotions. Each of us knows there are occasional patients who don't appear to be at the point where life will suddenly be over, but if you listen to the person carefully, there can be subtle clues he is ready to talk about dying. Most don't consciously know they are close to dying, but their inner self directs them to get into the subject. I try never to miss that moment because it may signal that there won't be another opportunity.

One day Jack began talking in an uncharacteristic way. "I know I can't last forever. I wonder just how bad it's going to be."

"Are you asking to talk about dying, Jack? Stop me if I'm wrong, but I have some thoughts I'd like to share with you, if that's what you want."

As I seized the opportunity I was keenly aware Linda was in the kitchen overhearing us without any chance to warn her. I knew this moment held great pain for her, too. I followed my usual pattern of asking what he knew about death, and not surprisingly, his concepts were interwoven with too many young people dying before their time with AIDS.

"Your body is the car you drive, Jack, and you are the driver. When the car breaks down and can't work anymore, the driver gets out and goes where he can have a vehicle that works." Jack studied my face intently, hanging onto every word.

I talked about near death experiences and some of the many stories I had personally heard. "I've know over thirty people who have had them, Jack, and in 1984 the Gallup poll identified over eight million people who have experienced near death and remembered it. That's a sizable number. Just think how many more have been added to that number since 1984. I can't tell you what to think. All I can do is share information with you and let you decide what to believe."

"In California I knew people who talked just like you do, Joy. Claimed they had beautiful experiences when they died, and their lives were never the same after that. From then on every day was special in a new way, but best of all, they were no longer afraid to die." Now that the door had been opened, Jack talked on about his beliefs. "I do believe life continues even after the body can't live. I guess I just don't know how to feel about the process."

"Death involves many aspects, Jack. There's the emotional pain of leaving loved ones, and we have to deal with the physical pain of a body that can be wracked with incredible hurting. We will be here to help you with both." We shared the concerns that laid so heavily on his mind.

"There's also a spiritual body which needs nourishment and we have unseen hands that guide us there, too. We are surrounded by love, both here and where we are going," I said.

"The angels." With that Jack began to cry, slow, sad tears that spilled over his lids and oozed down his tanned cheeks.

I called upon the words that comfort me when I must witness someone so young about to die. "We all have to remember our souls are in charge. The soul knows what it is doing, even if we don't understand. We can trust that and our Creator who loves us all. And I do mean all, Jack. Our Creator is very clear on how He loves everyone. It's man that is mixed up on the subject."

"I just want to know I won't be out of my mind." He sobbed. "I don't want to think I lost that! And I want to be here. I don't want to die in the hospital!"

"I can't promise you either of those two, Jack. Some things are out of my hands. I can promise you I will do my best to help you stay here and handle all the symptoms that develop, so you can be comfortable. I promise you I'll look after Linda and Michelle and everyone, and do my very best to see that they are all right so you don't have to worry. And I can promise you I'll never forget you or our wonderful times together."

His crying now slowly gave way to quiet reflection. "I know you will, Joy. Please look after Linda."

Gently stroking his arm, I felt my heart become heavy with my fear of helplessness for himself and Linda. "Anyway, it's not time yet, Jack. But we have to be prepared."

In the kitchen I mouthed, "I'm sorry," to Linda, my heart aching with concern for her, too. She nodded numbly. The next day when I called to be certain both were all right, she told me they had cried together after I left. "He's quiet today, but I know it had to be."

"And you, Linda? How are you doing?"

"I'm sad too, but I know you had to do it."

After that the joking in the household, which was always high, moved up a notch or two. The current subject was finding me a husband, and we had outrageous laughs as the ever-resourceful Linda came up with absurd suggestions. Like the true anchor she was, she held steady and kept everything strong for everyone else. She drew on her ability to lighten the tension with laughter. All talk of going to California gradually evaporated.

One day I came to visit and there were mischievous smiles on the faces of both Jack and Linda. Before I had time to figure out what was up, Linda instructed me, "Close your eyes and hold out your hands." Laughingly I followed the instructions, wondering what I would find.

"Oh, oh! This is an act of courage with you two. No telling what you've cooked up for me." Something soft and large was set into my hands and when I opened them there was the most gleeful witch on a broomstick I'd ever seen.

"So you won't forget our good times," Jack volunteered.

"She's wonderful! Gluwinda. I just know that's her name. I'm just hoping this isn't a caricature of me. Thank you! I am so touched." We laughed while I hugged my newly found witch. Jack's eyes sparkled with the fun of surprising me. For a few days we managed to feel almost normal, with the family carrying on their loving team effort to meet the challenges.

One day I arranged to meet Michelle for a Coke after school, somewhere I could talk with her out of the home. Patients are driven nuts by whisperings in another room out of their earshot. It signals to them that they are being protected from something and they become angry and afraid. Knowing that, I still needed to be certain where Michelle was with her own emotional adjustment, and a Coke break offered us the opportunity to talk alone.

"Yes, it's been hard," she said. "I see how sick Uncle Jack is now. I just try and be there for him and for my mom and dad. Like, they will go out when I'm home because they know I can handle it. I cry a lot sometimes and all that, but then I just get back to doing whatever I can."

"Michelle, you are fantastic! I wish I could clone this family and spread it around my caseload. How are you really doing? Do you have a good friend, or friends who know, and with whom you can talk about this?"

"Yeah, I have one best friend, Betsy. Like, she always understands. Most of my friends found out. I wasn't going to tell them because people have such mixed up attitudes about AIDS, and all that. But someone I confided in blurted it out to others. Man, I was so angry! You know, I didn't want anyone thinking awful things about Uncle Jack. He's such a sweetheart, and just because he got into wild behavior when he was young doesn't mean he's a terrible person."

"No, it doesn't, Michelle. Jack is a sweetheart who has done all kinds of things to help others. Do the guys give you a hard time?"

"Well, not most of them. Lots come up and say 'How's Uncle Jack doing?' and ask about him. If I'm real quiet some days there are always a few who say, 'Everything okay with Uncle Jack?' So, I guess, in the long run, it's working out all right. Like, I just ignore the others or tell them to shove it."

"Wow! Can this kid handle it?" I asked myself. "How I admire her. I couldn't imagine I was that mature at her age."

"Actually, it may have worked out better this way." Michelle paused, twirling a long strand of her auburn hair in her fingers. "Like, sometimes I see somebody taking real chances and doing things that really puts them at risk to get sick. People just don't take getting AIDS seriously. If they could see what I see!" She shook her head sadly and shuddered. "I take them aside and say, 'Are you crazy or something? Do you want to get AIDS? Take it from me you're being really stupid to do dangerous stuff.' Mostly they listen to me, so, I guess I've been able to help some people. I do feel good about that."

"Michelle, I really admire you." She blushed. "I'm going to count on you to let me know if the going gets tough, so I can help you. Also, if anyone else in the family starts to have a rough time, you give me a call. I'll come right over." We ended our visit with a hug.

Jack turned forty just before Halloween. "I just hope he doesn't die on his birthday," said Linda. "I don't know if I could take that!"

Searching for the right gifts was a problem, for what does one who is dying need? And yet we wanted to give Jack presents that showed him how much we cared. Linda found an exquisite ceramic Christmas tree with winsome teddy bears all over the branches. She placed it in his room and turned on its lights when his eyes were closed, so he would see the shining tree when he opened his eyes.

His birthday was on Saturday, and I drove in from my home to give him a gift. "If ever there were a time to visit a patient on my day off this is it," I said to myself as I drove. "Jack needs to know I see his beauty within."

I had selected a ceramic bell with an angel on top. "To call the angels whenever you need them," I said, for often our talk had turned to the angels and angel stories. I ate a piece of birthday cake as we chatted.

Blessedly, Jack felt well and energetic for his birthday. There really are miracles if we are just watching and calling them by their correct names, I thought.

Next, we made it through Halloween, with Jack weaker and sleeping more, but able to enjoy the costumes and visitors who trouped in to see the decorations. One set of holiday decorations came down, and another's went up. Thanksgiving coexisted joyfully with Christmas in all the places where Halloween had so recently hung. Now turkeys, pilgrims, bowls of gourds and clumps of corn stalks nestled between lighted trees, angels, and plump snowmen, while blinking stars transformed the ceilings into a sparkling night sky.

Jack began to pick at his food, and leave his favorite foods on the plate barely touched. Coco seldom left the bed, unless I moved her out for a bit, while I did the procedures requiring some sterile dressings. I knew the dog's constant presence signaled the pain was more intense. As gently as possible I pursued that with Jack.

"Yeah, Joy. It's the worst it's been," he admitted.

"We can deal with that by giving you more medicine, Jack. No need to bite the bullet in silence."

"I don't like to make it harder for everyone else, so I try not to complain," he said.

"Think of it as communication instead of complaining. That will help you remember you are simply honoring the truth," I said. I felt a wave of tenderness for Jack, because he tried so hard not to make things more difficult for us.

Even though he could eat little now, Linda prepared Jack's favorite foods so he could at least nibble at them. We knew his eyesight was failing. He slept more often and for longer periods of time, and we started crossing our fingers he would live to see the holidays he loved so much. Our favorite doctor began to make house calls. His wonderful presence meant strength, hope, and caring to Jack and, as sick as he was, Jack would glow during and after his visits. It was a boost no one else could have provided.

Jack began to give away a few prize possessions. His favorite cowboy boots, barely worn, went to a friend who had been thoughtful and supportive to him while he was still well enough to work. That touch of human decency had helped Jack hang on to his pride and humanity, and had made an incredible difference to him. Now he wanted to acknowledge that, in his own way. Clearly this was not to be left to chance.

"That's so thoughtful, Jack. Also so very like you." I smiled.

"So many people don't know what to say, so they just don't say or do anything. Dave never did that. He'd always ask if there was anything he could do, and if he thought I looked tired, he'd make me sit down and carry on for some time by himself. You don't forget people like that, Joy. They make all the difference. I had to say thanks in some way."

Not that all of our days were sad. Linda kept up a relentless pitch of suggestions to find me a husband. "I should introduce you to Jake, my butcher. Just think. If you go out with him, he may give you free pork chops."

"I didn't know I looked that hungry, Linda." Shaking laughter came from Jack, who enjoyed his nurse in the hot seat of Linda's creative kidding.

One day, when I arrived for my visit, there was another gift. This time it was a plaque with a paper mache doctor on it for my wall. "Since you're not cooperating with my great suggestions, I decided to find you a man you can't refuse." Linda's mischievous eyes sparkled. But the gleeful laughter coming from the bed was the best of all. Looking over I saw heaving shoulders and the sheer delight on Jack's face and, for a moment, we all forgot just how serious life could become.

Time seemed to increase in speed, and as we watched, Jack's ups and downs became our only constant. We held our breath after a bad day and wondered, "Is this it?" On good days we would feel a tenuous reprieve. By Thanksgiving we knew Jack's life would soon be over. To lose him on a holiday would be terrible. The indignity of dying on a day of joy struck at our hearts.

"You call me if it happens," I said to Linda and gave them my home phone number. I telephoned the evening and weekend on-call supervisors for my agency to update them on his condition. "I want to know right away. The family may need my help. By now I know them so well."

Jack remained calm and bravely endured the pain, and I knew our talks had helped him to find peace. At times he became confused, unaware of time or date, and his words would ramble, yet he remained calm. He told me, "I'm tired, Joy. So tired." We talked sparingly to save his strength.

"How long do I have?" he occasionally asked.

"As long as it takes for everything to be ready," I said. "Remember, you are not alone and you have but to ask for strength from God."

Privately, Linda worried about staying strong for the painful time ahead. Her drawn, sad face was carefully kept from Jack's view, as she struggled to stay the steadfast anchor she had chosen to be for him.

Jack managed to get through Thanksgiving to the immense relief of his family and me. He was quiet, but peaceful. When the end did come I was not there. On Saturday night, with all his family around him, Jack went into a tranquil sleep from which he never awakened. Linda kept watch through the night while others slept. When he died in the early morning hours, she had her quiet moments with him before she awoke the other family members.

The call came as I had requested. How it ends is out of our control to predict. At least Jack got his wish to die at home, was my first thought, followed by I don't think any of us could bear it if he had to go back to the hospital and died there.

"Tell me what happened, Linda. Are you all right?" I asked when I got to the house. Talking about it is pivotal to coming out of shock and beginning the slow process of moving on, and it was important that this incredible caregiver be at peace about the final moments.

"He was real quiet, breathing slowly. He hadn't said much all evening, just slept a lot. He didn't want much to eat. We were all here. I wondered if this was going to be it, or what. You know, it's terrible waiting for the moment to happen! I prayed it wouldn't be hard for him." Linda paused, her eyes dry. But her face telegraphed her heart was heavy with sadness at the loss of her best friend, the buddy whose life she guarded for such a long time.

"It was in the night. I was the one watching him. He just stopped breathing. A couple of times I thought this might be it, but he would breathe again. Finally, he simply didn't take another breath."

I nodded in sympathy, reaching out my hand to lightly squeeze her arm just above the elbow. Sometimes there are no words that will speak as eloquently as silence.

"But I had my quiet time with him, time to say good-bye and do what I had to do. I needed that. Waking everyone up any sooner wasn't going to help anyone." The ever-practical Linda had thought of everyone else, even at this heart-wrenching moment. "The hardest part was when they came and took him away. I worked so hard to protect him! It just drove home to me how I couldn't really make the difference. He never wanted to leave here and that hurts."

"I know, Linda. That is the very hardest part for many. You may not have been able to hold back the disease, but neither can anyone else. And Linda, you held life together for him all these years. That must not get lost in the shuffle now that the sadness is so intense." She nodded slowly, her face a mask of sadness. I turned to Michelle. "You really all right?"

"Now Uncle Jack doesn't have to be in pain any more." Her calm accepting face backed up the statement, so I could see she meant it.

"I see Coco is having a rough time." The dog was in the corner and had not bounded over to greet me as he usually did.

"He won't go near the room. He won't eat and just lies there. He lost his buddy, too." Linda's sad face became softer as she obviously felt tenderness for her dog's grief.

For the successive weeks, I stayed in as close contact as I could, without taking away their freedom to grieve in their own ways. Balancing the needs of the survivors to have their quiet time with being there really requires listening to what they say, and responding to your own sensitivities. Knowing them, like I did, I tried to be a comfort to them but I was also a reminder of the painful time we had spent together. My conversations with Jack echoed in my mind. "You promised Jack you'd help Linda. Somehow you have to find the right balance, here, Joy or else it doesn't work."

Linda had days when she wondered what more she could have done. "You are going through the 'if onlys,' Linda." I reminded her gently, but persistently, of the great gift of love she had given. "It never feels good enough, but I have never seen anyone do a better job than you have done. Don't take your eyes off that for a moment. You did everything possible and more!" I tried to reassure her.

"It doesn't feel good enough," she said. "Not nearly good enough."

"There are always 'if onlys' to go through. It's a very little talked about stage of grief. Whatever is your 'if only' now, had that been accomplished you would simply have a different 'if only,'" I went on.

Linda shuddered. "I wonder how life will ever get back to normal again."

"Learning to accept the unacceptable changes us. There is no way to avoid this stage. As you face it, realize over again that you made every choice in as an informed and thorough manner as you could, each step of the process. There is no better way to do it than that." Words helped sustain her, at least a little, but just a little. Only time was going to make a substantial difference.

Sometimes I found her with pain that was overwhelming. "The pain is not a measure of how well you are doing or not doing, Linda. It is a measure of how much you care. You are doing very well and it is extremely painful because you love him so much. One doesn't cancel out the other."

"I can't imagine I'll ever get back to not missing him, Joy."

"You lost not only Jack, but your very schedule. There is no way to be happy about either." She nodded.

In the final analysis it took what it always takes, time to adjust to the unacceptable. Each family member grieved in his own way and according to his own time schedule. Gradually, their lives found new momentum, as each found a way to focus once more on living. The incredible strength Linda possessed came through for her journey through grieving as it had always been present to anchor Jack.

Time brought fresh perspective for me, too. But there's something about Halloween every year that makes me chuckle and remember a Halloween that coexisted side by side with Christmas.

As for Gluwinda, she hangs in my living room where I can look up every day and smile when I see her outrageous face. Then I remember a wonderful time with Jack and his anchor, who sustained us all, and I know I was truly lucky to have been his nurse.

Compassion

*While I thought that I was learning how to live, I have been
learning how to die.*

~ Leonardo Da Vinci

The tall sturdy man with a ruddy complexion answered
the doorbell. He had an almost jovial expression on his face,
as he graciously welcomed me with a broad sweep of his
hand in from the heavy snowstorm. In a broken accent he
said, "Come... in."

"I am the nurse who has come to see Raisa. Am I in the
right home?" I asked.

"Nurse. Ahhh," he replied with his thick accent. I wondered what to do next. A handsome young man, about twenty years old, appeared as if by magic, and gestured for me to
follow him with a sweep of the hand that led me to the stairs,
as he said a simple, "Please." It was encouraging to see I was
expected, as I had begun to suspect I would have the challenge of communicating with people who understood very
little English. I followed as he led me to a bedroom at the top
of the stairs.

I looked around the room and saw two neatly made beds
with large pillows, dressed in cases with red, yellow and

green borders patiently fashioned from tidy, purposeful embroidery stitches with a distinctly Ukrainian theme. My gaze halted at one bed, where a very pale, thin young woman with dark hair spilling over the pillow and large serious, penetrating eyes looked back at me. I greeted her, and it was now clear: this was not an English speaking home.

I scanned my papers for the fine print that would tell me more about this family and learned that Raisa had come to my city from Russia with her family about a year ago. "This family must feel right at home with all the snow we're having. It looks like a Russian winter out there to me," I said to myself.

Some things are universal in sign language, but starting the paper work for a homecare case is not one of them. Slowly and laboriously I set about finding words that could have meaning for someone limited in English.

"How do you feel?" I tried.

The shrug and discouraged expression led me to believe Raisa understood what I said, but lacked enough command of the language to describe her condition and tell me just how ill she felt. Gamely we grappled back and forth, with attempts on both of our parts to solve this dilemma, but we made little progress. At the sound of heavy Russian words behind me, I turned to look directly into the eyes of a strong, towering woman, complete with kerchief, talking earnestly with her son. This must be Raisa's mother, I thought. I wished I understood what she was saying. It sounded like directions.

Suddenly the brother dashed up the flight of stairs that I quickly surmised was an attic access to the other side of the house, and returned with a young woman, dressed in a simple dirndl skirt, who, like her mother, in the custom of her country, wore a matching babushka.

"Hello, I am sister," said the friendly voice. "I help?" she inquired.

English! At least now I could get on with opening Raisa to homecare. As a community health nurse I needed some details. My agency and the insurance companies insisted on them. I could have arranged for an interpreter, but that takes knowing one is needed ahead of time. I wonder why no one thought to warn me?

We quickly made progress with the essentials. After introducing ourselves to each other, I gamely made several futile attempts to pronounce the sister's Russian name. "You can call me Katia," she said, choking back her amusement. No doubt she had encountered the struggle often enough that she had found a pronounceable substitute that worked in her new country. I said to myself, "No one ever accused me of being a natural with foreign languages. At least I can manage Katia."

I busied myself examining Raisa, taking her temperature, blood pressure, and listening to her lungs. All the while I remained painfully aware she was only twenty-two years old and had severe lung cancer. Casually, I asked, "Where in Russia are you from?"

"Near Chernobyl," said Katia. All heads nodded in solemn agreement.

"Chernobyl?" I was in shock. I thought, Dear God, this is one of the victims of Chernobyl.

I tried to appear calm while my mind was in a whirl provoked by the word. I was thankful for my medical training that had taught me to stay calm and deal with emotions later, but my thoughts raced fast and furiously as I dealt with this most unexpected turn of events.

I'd been in Finland a few weeks after the great Chernobyl disaster and knew how the radiation, carried by the winds, had poisoned many reindeer in Norway and other nearby Scandinavian countries. Reindeer meat was a staple in the Scandinavian diet, and I had witnessed firsthand one of the far-reaching effects of this disaster, disruption of the food source. Television accounts periodically reported on the devastation and trauma, which uprooted a whole segment of the Russian people, none of whom were warned in a timely enough manner to assure their safety. Now, I remembered news reports of the dramatically increased thyroid cancer rate among residents for hundreds of miles around Chernobyl. It was well noted and studied in medical circles.

This sudden cascade of thoughts, tumbling one on top of another, engulfed my mind, in a vane attempt to cushion the shocking images flashing before my eyes.

One of my friends had been a missionary in Russia just a year before. She visited the wards of the hospitals to see the little children full of cancer, casualties of the radiation fall-out. She came to hug them, pin an angel pin on each one, and place pretty bracelets around their wrists to let them know they were not forgotten. Pictures she had shown me had lodged in my brain and I worked to hold back the flood of emotions so suddenly triggered. The overwhelming sadness and grief my friend felt, when she returned, was something I will never forget. No matter how I appeared calm and centered, I was feeling that sadness now. And I realized how serious Raisa's condition was.

Katia fetched a map, and I came out of my solemnity to study it. We established they'd lived two to three hundred miles from the center of the disaster. I took Raisa's pulse and counted her respirations, finding some comfort in familiar routines while struggling to steady my heart, now flooded with sorrowful images of children, with enormous eyes in emaciated frames, struggling to understand what fate had handed them. Little by little I gained all the information permitted by our limited capacity to talk.

"How's her breathing?" I asked, speaking slowly.

"Not good some days," said Katia, her controlled expression offering few clues.

"Has oxygen been ordered?"

"Ox...i..?" She looked puzzled.

I pantomimed the equipment, my hands flailing in the air as I talked. "It's about this big, on wheels, has a long tube and some of the tubing goes on her face."

"Ahhh. Yes, in other room," Katia answered. With a beckoning gesture she led me to the room next door.

"You understand how to use this?" I asked. "Does she need it very often?"

Katia shrugged, as she nodded and said, "I know," leaving me to wonder if she understood either question. I thought, Maybe I'd better teach her in case she really doesn't understand.

Speaking very slowly, I attempted to instruct Katia on use of the oxygen equipment, and the need for keeping the portable unit near Raisa, in case she needed help quickly. Seeing the blank look my instructions brought, my heart sank. I needed to get an interpreter over here fast, I thought.

I finished the examination and completed as much of the paperwork as I could. After we set another date for me to visit, I gathered my clipboard, zipped up my bag and prepared to brave the storm one more time. I mused to myself,

"This has been a most interesting beginning. Wonder what is in store for me on this case?"

Subsequent visits went smoothly enough, if I detached from needing to know every detail. Someone always fetched Katia through the attic. Her English was the best in the house, but even at that, we really couldn't make each other understand everything that was being said. It was patently obvious, however, that loving family care did much to hold back the devastation of a rapidly progressing disease. To my surprise, we had several visits where Raisa held her own in a way I dared not hope could happen.

I worked with an interpreter on some visits. She knew the family and filled me in on some of Raisa's history. That allowed me to cut through some of the mysterious aspects of caring for my precious charge and create some deeper understandings of how to proceed. Gradually we found our way around our language differences and struck a balance that allowed me to feel I could stay on top of the situation, at least for the present.

Katia, her husband, and their three children had been in the United States for a year and a half, a little longer than the remainder of the family, and they lived in the other side of the double house. The family had been sponsored to our city by a relative who was a very active member of the Russian Reformed Church. Katia's fourth child, a three-month-old daughter, had been born here. One day she brought her baby along to visit while I was checking Raisa. The plump, angelic three-month-old was dressed in a pink flowered dress with a matching kerchief on her head. Her winsome smile, with toothless gums, was contagious. I laughed aloud. There was no way to experience her joy and not smile. What a saving grace it must be to have such ready laughter in this somber household, I thought.

Raisa would smile at the baby, the smile taking charge of her lean and serious face and exposing her gold filled teeth. Briefly her deep eyes would sparkle as she cuddled the child, drawn in momentarily by her magical innocence. Then silently Raisa would hand the baby back, all sparkle draining from her face, the contrast between her reality and this baby too large to bridge for any length of time. Her mother, who knew no English, hung in the background, babushka-covered head bowed slightly, sadly watching the interaction.

My visits assumed an ongoing serious vein that, try as I might, I could not relieve. My feeble attempts at some Russian words were as close as we came to humor. "It almost makes me want to keep trying Russian to bring some comic relief here. How I wish I could do more," I said to myself.

Katia did her best to be on hand and usually was accompanied by four-year-old, blond Alexander, who was very well behaved and just as serious as his mother.

"It doesn't seem right," I said to my daughter, Carol, one day. "Something good needs to happen for these children to step out of that non-stop sadness. I picked up a colorful teething ring for the baby, but do you happen to have a toy I can take to Alex? We need a change of pace to relieve the drama at least temporarily."

"Oh, Mom! How hard! Let's look in my cupboard of things I've put away for the future. I must have an appropriate toy. It's too sad not to do something." I knew I could count on her kind heart, and sure enough, she produced a moveable small truck, with parts that could be dismantled and put back together again. "Just take it for him. I'm so glad to help," she said. "I think of my own small ones and can't imagine what it must be like to have to deal with all that!"

Arriving now, with the small surprises tucked into my bag between the blood pressure cuff and wrapped bandages, I stalled for time with small talk, awaiting the arrival of Katia to interpret. Shortly, she came down through the attic, with Alex and the baby in tow. I reached into my medical bag and retrieved the gifts. "For you, Alex," I said. Hesitantly he took the truck, looking to his mother for permission to receive it. Katia nodded, with a small smile, and Alex broke into a gigantic grin. Immediately he dropped to the floor and began wheeling the truck across the tiles. The baby took the teething keys and promptly stuck them in her large toothless grin, as we all laughed aloud. For at least a brief time, our day was filled with smiles and laughter.

As much joy as the baby brought, the levity was short lived. Only a few visits later it was apparent that Raisa was not doing well. She had to be sent to the hospital emergency department more than once for painful procedures to release her breathing. Word came back to me that her lung x-ray showed "white out," a condition wherein the disease has spread so prevalently, that the lungs appear only as white on film, looking like a snowstorm. Definitely not a good sign, I thought. Now what?

Then came one of the times when I wrestled with the results of my examination. Raisa's lungs were not exchanging air well, as confirmed by my stethoscope. It was becoming a judgment call on how to proceed. On the surface, Raisa's breathing showed little deterioration from her usual pattern. Not that her breathing was ever very good. But clearly there was decline. I decided to report the symptom to her doctor.

"I'm not certain how to proceed. On the one hand she doesn't look much different, but her lungs are as tight as I have heard, and there isn't much air exchanged," I said to the doctor.

"Let's sit tight a little longer and observe her," said the doctor. "We may have to send her in again, but if we watch carefully, we might be able to avoid another hospitalization. She's such a high risk to catch something infectious in the hospital. That could make her die even sooner, she's so weak." Grateful for the clear direction, I agreed to give it some more time. In my heart I felt certain we would not have long to wait.

I said to myself, "This is the point, Joy, where you usually sit down and talk with the family about their understanding of the disease, their hopes, and dreams. What are you going to do make that happen with this language barrier? It's pretty clear there isn't the luxury of much time." I made plans to call our interpreter as well as to place an immediate referral for a social worker to assist the family with understanding the gravity of our situation. I scheduled a visit for all of us to talk three days later.

Meanwhile, I rehearsed Katia one more time with instructions on oxygen use and emergency on-call procedures. Privately I worried. Man, I hope she understands these emergency procedures! We're in deep trouble if she's said yes to me and doesn't really know what I meant, I thought.

The next day was blustery with heavy snow and howling winds. The sunlight that managed to peek from behind the heavy dark clouds turned the terrain into a bright and eerie landscape, complete with whiteouts of blowing snow. It would have been breathtakingly beautiful if it hadn't been so

treacherous for travel. It was white knuckle driving at best.
"Absolutely necessary visits only" were directed by my
agency.

I mused to myself, "When roads are in emergency conditions, so are many people's health. Must be Murphy's Law.
Today, with this huge barometric pressure drop there's
bound to be an emergency somewhere. Sure hope I'll be
able to get there!"

My car phone rang in early afternoon. "Can you get right
over to Raisa's house? Her sister called and she can't
breathe," said the secretary in our office.

I felt my heart sink. "Were you able to determine how
bad this is? I mean, do we need to call an ambulance or
what? It's terrible out here! I don't know how quickly I can
get there."

"Could you call? It's really hard to understand her. Maybe
you can tell that better than I can. The accent is awfully
thick and she sounded frightened," the secretary answered.

No kidding, I thought. What makes anyone think I'll be
any better at understanding this? I sure hope I've figured out
enough of the accent to handle this, as it sounds serious.

My call determined that Raisa was indeed having
difficulty with breathing. Katia sounded stressed and kept
saying, "You come. You come," over and over. Our phone
conversations were always limited. This time was no excep-
tion. My attempts to instruct Katia how to call an ambulance met with failure. I couldn't make her understand my
questions enough to determine how critical Raisa's situation had become. And sign language, my most powerful
tool, was totally lost to me in this situation. Our slowly
improving communication obviously didn't include the
telephone.

Never, absolutely never before had Katia insisted I come at once. With a heavy heart, I reassured her I would do something and called back the office.

"Anyone from our department there?" I asked. There was one nurse, Sue. "Put her on the phone, would you?"

"Sue, I'm about to ask the biggest favor possible." I gave her a one-minute summary of the situation. "Would you be willing to go to Raisa's house while I try to get there as fast as possible? I have no idea how long it'll take as I'm outside the city. It may take two of us to sort this out anyway, as this family really isn't in a position to decide on this one. I know it's the worst day of the year out there, and I'm not trying to dump this on you, but this girl's only twenty-two."

"I'm on my way." she replied.

Everyone with any sense was off the highway. I was now on a limited access expressway that was unusually clear of traffic and miraculously less snowy than some of the surrounding areas. There was something to be said for the wind when it blew in the direction that helped instead of hindered. I pulled out the stops and drove as fast, within the speed limit, as I felt safe to do. Maybe I will pick up a police escort, I thought. I need to get there without becoming a casualty myself. Why is it there is never a police car when you really want one? Struggling to keep down my own feelings to a place where I could just react, I pushed through the snowy terrain that did nothing to shore up my sagging confidence, or avert my rapidly growing sense of dread.

My car swung into the snowy driveway and I realized I was stuck in a drift. No matter. I can deal with this later, I thought. Impatiently I plowed through drifts above my knees to reach the door, and ran up the stairs. One look at Raisa told me the answer I had dreaded. She was in acute respiratory distress, gasping for air, panic written all over her gaunt face. Her eyes, always huge, pled with me for help as she lay stoically on the bed enduring her fate.

Pulling pillows from the beds as I moved, I sat Raisa upright, pushing the pillows behind her to give her support. Dashing into the adjoining room, I pulled the emergency oxygen tank toward her. "Raisa, do this." I breathed slowly and deliberately to show her more controlled breathing, and then I placed the oxygen tubing on her face and continued to breathe every breath with her. For once sign language was the language of choice.

A sea of serious faces gathered around us. Raisa's mother sat on the second bed, the back of her knuckles against her mouth, stifling the protest and fear she felt. Katia studied my every move, no doubt measuring my performance against her own, and my heart went out to her. How inadequate she must have felt! Glancing back at Raisa, I noted little improvement with her breathing, and I swung back to the oxygen tank control, moving it to the highest setting just as Sue arrived.

"How on earth did you get here so fast?" she asked. Sizing up the situation instantly, she went straight to Raisa's stricken mother, and placing her arms around her, sat beside her on the bed. Silently she shared the pain we were so helpless to remove as she sought to comfort a mother she had never met, but so instantly understood. I placed the emergency call through 911 and asked for an ambulance at once. I knew I could count on the skill of the highly trained crew and that they would find their way through the storm to help us. Finally I allowed myself the luxury of the few moments it took to take off my coat.

I bent to Raisa, kneeling on the floor to be nearer to her.

This was not a time to struggle with language. I stroked her
arm and gently, but lovingly, placed what I hoped was a reassuring arm around her shoulders, breathing each breath
with her and showing her how to slow down her rate. I held
her hand in mine and smiled into her eyes. I said slowly, a
breath between each word, "You are doing fine. Just keep
breathing slowly," as I let my actions do what words could
not.

"Pack a few things for her," I said to Katia. "Her housecoat, toothbrush, whatever she might want with her." She
did not respond, except to pick up the brush and comb by
Raisa's bedside, while I continued the effort to ease Raisa's
tortured breathing.

The siren sounded more like a fire engine. Before we had
time to fathom that, two firemen with emergency equipment were bursting up the stairs. In my concern for Raisa I
had forgotten the fire department arrives to back up each
ambulance call, in case their emergency training is needed.
Because they can usually get there more quickly, they were
first on the scene. The startled faces of the family registered
fear. Ah, yes. Not long ago they lived where authorities
could burst in and it meant danger, I thought.

"My name's Joy and I am the community health nurse
who visits Raisa. She is having trouble breathing, and so I
called for the ambulance. She'll be all right until they arrive;
I need you to step back and not frighten her. The family just
came from Russia, so they don't know our procedures, and
right now, the whole thing is very scary for all of them."

Graciously responding to my authority, they stepped back
and allowed me to continue my efforts. "It's all right," I tried
to reassure the family. "They are here to help and we are
safe." I smiled my gratitude to the firemen and silently

thanked God for understanding firemen who protect us all in all kinds of weather.

No sooner had I recovered from that challenge and there were three more people dashing up the stairs. Led by one very active and vocal medic, the ambulance crew began barking out orders and an oxygen facemask was hastily placed on Raisa's face. Stricken eyes full of terror looked out at me, around the white plastic dome with its blue straps now tightened around her face. I knew an oxygen mask was the treatment of choice in such a situation, but Raisa's now uncontrolled panic would cancel any benefit we would gain from it. My heart sank. Is it my imagination or did her breathing rate just double? This will never do! I thought.

One swift glance at the terrified faces of the whole family, while they struggled to maintain their trust in me and hold steadfast in the face of the personal danger they felt, told me I must move fast. The panicked look in their eyes made it patently clear, we were approaching pandemonium.

There are times when a nurse must over-ride everyone. I knew my ambulance crew was well trained and had responded in deplorable conditions with great speed to help us. I did the one thing I knew I must and pulled rank.

"Back off!" I said with authority in my voice. "She doesn't speak the language and shouting questions is just making her breathing worse. Deal with me and I will give you what you need to know." I ripped all the information they would need from my travel folder and handed it over to the crew. Directing the emergency care in a fully commanding tone, I issued firm, concise, and direct orders. The oxygen mask was removed and the less threatening tubing reinstated. To their credit, the emergency crew responded peacefully to my requests, every one of them backing off and deferring to my directions.

Looking reassuringly into Raisa's eyes while squeezing her hands I tried to comfort her. "You go. It'll be all right. Katia will go too, and I'll come see you." Knowing that touch can be the universal communicator, I placed every bit of confidence I could into that squeeze. She looked back at me with trust and nodded.

Katia ran to get her coat. "Let her ride in the ambulance with her sister," I instructed the ambulance crew. "If you need information she has the best English and she will be the only one who can reassure Raisa, if you need help en route."

As quickly as the house had been full of strangers it now emptied. Her father and brother decided to accompany Raisa, too, and bustled off to put on their fur hats and heavy parkas. Sue left to carry on with her work.

Now alone and bewildered, in the empty bedroom so recently the scene of our life and death struggle, Raisa's mother sat, staring desolately at the tussled bed with its brightly embroidered pillowcases, no longer able to caress the dark haired Raisa.

She had stayed home to care for the little ones, her lack of English the finger of fate that left her behind, while her daughter fought for her life out of her sight and away from her touch. She could no longer hold back her tears. The sobs began quietly at first, tears of anguish falling among heart breaking sounds.

I reached her side and wrapped her as best I could in my arms, hugging her tightly. I held her, while the pain of being a mother who could do nothing, spilled out in heart-wrenching sobs. Gradually the sounds of anguish subsided.

Placing her hands out, palms up, she shrugged sadly, as if to say 'What is there to do?' I looked at her, my heart hurting, understanding the language of one mother to another. How can I reach her? Can she really see how much I care? I wondered.

Silently I placed my hands together in the universal gesture of prayer and nodded towards her. "Ah," she said and joined her hands together. Looking up, she nodded as I said, "Pray." We held our hands in prayerful positions for a minute, locked in understanding that joined us at last.

"Pray," she said tenuously, and I watched her emotions calm at the realization this was something she could do. We prayed silently, each in our own way, for the safety of Raisa, who was only twenty-two and in need of a miracle.

We held our bond of mutual understanding and caring for many minutes. Time seemed to be moving both devastatingly slowly and rushing disastrously quickly at the same moment. She was struggling gallantly to grasp the seriousness of the crisis that had just unfolded before our eyes and make sense of it. Conflicting emotions vied for our attention as, each in our own way, we desperately searched for hopeful thoughts to comfort us.

I prepared to go, reluctant to leave her alone with her fear. I moved out the door and into the storm—torn by my desire to wrap her in caring strong enough to lift her from the wrench of her pain, and my conflicting need to move on with my work—and left her to do the one thing that remained for her to do. Numbed by the pain of life just witnessed, I hardly felt the ravages of winter that greeted me once more. Getting my car out of a snowdrift will seem like a piece of cake after all this, I thought.

Raisa was admitted to the hospital intensive care unit.

Katia was openly relieved. The responsibility for being family caretaker and spokesperson was beginning to weigh heavily upon her. She had done a noble job, but now the prognosis was not good, and we knew it. All of my hopes for helping them were now pinned on the meeting we had scheduled.

The day of our meeting arrived and for a change, it was not snowing. Maryanne, our social worker, and I entered the house and were ushered into the living room. A circle of chairs faced the doorway, and there, I was startled to see six adult men, whom I had never met, waiting for us with the family. We learned they were good friends from the church who had come to help their friends adjust to the tragedy, and most likely to help them ascertain if we were on the up and up. Clearly this is a culture where the men have reigned, I thought. How remarkable it must seem to them to turn things over to Katia because she has the best English.

We began the painful task of helping them all adjust, as every word we uttered was translated patiently by our now familiar interpreter. "As you know, Raisa is very ill. There is much we can do, but some times when the disease becomes very advanced in spite of our best efforts, the patient does not get better. Raisa is now at that point." I paused to let the interpreter catch up. We artfully paced ourselves to each other's needs, as the social worker and I began the task of helping them understand, falling naturally into a smooth rhythm. I was grateful Maryanne and I had worked together on many cases, and now we drew on our established teamwork.

We told them about the stages of grieving, and what we might expect in the days and weeks ahead for Raisa. I hoped there would be weeks, but I doubted it. To them I said,

"There is no guarantee of how much time there is to be."
The interpreter added what must have been information of
her own, as her explanations took much longer than our
words. Stoically they received our sad message.

One of the male visitors asked, "Would it have made any
difference if she had been in another city or country when
she became ill?" We reassured them no one in the world
knows how to reverse damage so severe.

"Katia has done a wonderful job," I said, turning to
acknowledge her. It was important to lessen the pain of
inadequacy she must have been feeling. Out of the corner
of my eye I saw her smile with pride and noticeably relax. I
thought, I hope saying this in front of everyone will help
you know you've done well, so when it's over, you won't
wonder what you could have done better.

"You all are doing things just right. But there are no better ways we know to help those like Raisa at this point. With
all we have learned in medicine, we have so much more to
discover."

Pausing to let the interpreter impart my words, I studied
the serious faces all locked studiously upon her, and slowly
nods punctuated their understanding.

We let them see our sorrow and reassured them we were
there for them. We answered their questions as honestly and
gently as we could, but we honored them with the truth as
we saw it.

At the end they told us through their interpreter, "You
have good hearts. We know you have done what you can
to help. We are glad we are here with you." The usually
stoic Katia had tears in her eyes as we hugged and said
good-bye, and we held the embrace for a full moment,
reluctant to break the bond we had established, forged as it
was out of necessity and heartbreak.

Raisa remained in the hospital. When Katia had hurried-
ly packed Raisa's belongings to go to the hospital, I had
instructed her to pack a housecoat. When that didn't happen after I requested it twice, I realized it wasn't language
barrier. She had none. My strong conviction that Raisa
needed a message of her special-ness before it was too late,
led me to the nearest discount store, where I settled on a
warm and fuzzy fuchsia robe with delicate embroidered
flowers on a lace collar. The bill was just over ten dollars
with the sale markdown. What could I possibly hope to
achieve with ten dollars that could do as much good as the
caring I hope this small gift can convey? At least I thought
of it while she's still with us.

At home, I selected the happiest flowered paper and
brightest bow I could find, determined to cheer up Raisa in
whatever limited fashion that remained, and wrapped the
package for her. I arrived at the hospital just in time to find
her being transferred out of the intensive care unit to a regular floor, belongings and medical equipment piled at the
foot of the stretcher. I grabbed one end of the stretcher and
helped move her into her new room. I also helped lift her
into bed, shuffling the pillows behind her head to settle her
as comfortably as possible.

For once she had abandoned the kerchief, and as she lay
in bed, weakened and quiet with oxygen tubing in place, her
dark, wavy hair framed her frail face and spilled over the pillow. I thought how alone she must feel. She was in a new
country, away from her family and surrounded by those who
communicate with her as I do, mostly through sign language, warm smiles and gentle touching. I said to myself,
"Wonder if I'll ever see you again, Raisa? You're breathing
easier but I know that look, and it tells me there isn't much
more time."

"For you. Open it!" I smiled what I hoped was my most cheery smile and handed her the brightly wrapped package. Her incredulous look and bright eyes needed no interpretation. I watched her meticulously break each piece of scotch tape, careful not to rip the paper, which she obviously planned to be used again. She lifted out the warm and cheery robe, her look of wonder and joyous disbelief saying it all. I thought, How often what is so much to receive is so very little to give. That smile of joy is worth a million dollars, Raisa, and I'll never forget it.

Thoughts of Raisa intruded on everything I did after I left her side. I knew there was nothing more for me to do, but something drew me back to her a few days later. I needed to see for myself what was happening to her. She lay in the bed in coma, head elevated to ease her breathing, oxygen tubing in place. Her family surrounded her in quiet vigil. Her mother sat close to the bed touching Raisa's still hand. Kerchiefed young women from the church prayed silently, and hugged and comforted the family members. Raisa's brother arrived with his big Russian fur hat that matched the fur collar on his coat, and he looked tall and stately as he stood by the bed. His lean and handsome face distorted with sadness, as he looked helplessly at his sister. His brow knitted and his eyes darkened with pain, as he bravely fought to hold back his grief. Raisa's father's usually jovial face was now lined with wrinkles that had aged him fifteen years. All trace of hope was gone from his tall and sturdy frame, and his face held only unspeakable sadness laced with the stoic acceptance only time and the endurance of having to take life as it comes can teach one.

Silently but ardently I was hugged, each one holding me tightly, as if to hang on to the feelings we shared and cling to the time that was left. Church members with better English thanked me for helping Raisa and the family. "Thank you for your caring heart," they said, as we shared our tears for young Raisa, whose only crime was she had lived in the shadow of a nuclear disaster.

I left her hospital room that day, knowing I would not see Raisa again. I stopped to talk with the nurses on the unit and found them fighting back their own tears. It is the largest affront of all to have entered medicine to help save people, only to find that with all the medical world can offer, there is nothing that can be done to save someone so young. All we could do was be there for each other, knowing we all felt the inadequacy of our efforts and hoping we could lighten the pain each other felt with our sharing. I requested they call to tell me when Raisa's fight was over, and left my home phone number.

The phone call came just four hours later and told me, all too soon, what I had known I would hear. Raisa had died that snowy afternoon, surrounded by her loving family and the babushka wearing members of her church, in a hospital room in her new country, in spite of the tubes and shiny emergency equipment, and in spite of the nurses and doctors who cried as they silently did their very best.

Good-bye, Raisa, I thought, as I hung up the phone. I will never forget you and your courage. It'll be easy to breathe again where you are now. And everyone will be able to understand you, even without English. You've just moved to the land of universal language. But there'll always be a part of you, right here, warm and safe in my heart until we meet again.

Forgiveness

Forgiveness is the aroma of a violet on the heel that has crushed it.

~ Ram Dass

The impressive five-story brick apartment building, a relic from a more opulent era now past, was tucked into a neighborhood lined with spacious structures and large gracious trees. I parked my car under a magnificent spreading oak tree that rustled a friendly greeting in the breeze, and found my way into the building. The creaking elevator, with open gate, lurched and inched its way to the third floor as I reflected on my assignment. "Go find out why this man, who was discharged from the hospital to go to the hospice unit, never arrived," my supervisor said. "He came north from Arizona where he spends winters, to spend his summer with family. He landed in the hospital and is so ill they decided he needs the inpatient unit. No one's heard from him since he left the hospital. Supposedly his liver is about to shut down, and he agreed to the hospice unit, then never showed up."

My phone call to introduce myself and announce I was coming for a visit had yielded no clues. I pulled back the accordion metal door as the elevator shuddered to a stop and considered what was about to unfold.

"Not very many people who are heading for the hospice unit go home instead," I said to myself. "Wonder what situation I'm walking into on this one." I crossed the darkened hallway and knocked on the door. Promptly I was welcomed into a comfortable apartment, neat and cheery with comfortable furnishings and a sparse but adequate kitchen. A petite and attractive woman, who looked much younger than the eighty years listed on my admission sheet, greeted me. Her neatly coifed hair framed a smile that was laced with tension, and the worried look in her eyes announced all was not well in the household.

Mario sat in a lounge chair, eyeing me with a mixture of curiosity and easy charm that belied the gravity of his illness. His solid frame and broad shoulders testified to the strength with which he encountered life, and his booming voice reinforced his forcefulness. I noted the jaundiced eyes and knew that he was experiencing much more than his bravado allowed him to acknowledge, even to himself. He must be a very good actor, I thought. It's hard to believe he's eighty-three years old, and he certainly doesn't look as sick as his lab values say he is. Wonder when the bottom will drop out of his good luck?

"So you're the nurse they've sent over to check on me. My daughter is a nurse, too. Have a seat," he said, graciously. "Charlotte," he growled, "get her a chair."

Charlotte sat quietly with hands folded in her lap in readiness to jump at his every command. She started to rise obediently, but I waved her back as I took the nearest seat. Her pleasant smile struggled to cover the anxiety Mario's latest defiant stand had created. Instantly, my heart went out to this gentle shy woman who sat in faithful attendance to her husband of sixty years.

"Is your daughter currently working as a nurse?" I asked.

"Oh, yes. Meredith works at a doctor's office or she'd be here now," Mario assured me. "She works three days a week."

"Where did you work when you lived here, Mario?" I asked.

Conversation was no problem for this take-charge man, who obviously had been a strong presence in every arena of his life. It came as no surprise to learn he had been a leader in the labor field, as his commanding authoritative manner demanded the respect usually accorded leaders. He had risen high in the union ranks by working hard all his life, although his background was one of poverty. "As the old-est of the family, I quit school and worked to provide for the rest of them. Times were hard and you had to be tough to make it back then. People have it too easy these days." He folded his arms across his chest. "I worked my way up through the ranks, the way you're supposed to do. No one handed it to me!" Mario's chin thrust forward a notch, making clear his strong determination and ability to work hard had helped him carve out a successful living in indus-try, more than compensating for his lack of education and opportunity.

I glanced at Charlotte and sensed she had provided the steady, patient, and loving balance that quietly made order out of the chaos of his volatile actions. No doubt she won-dered how she was going to pick up the pieces this time.

"Tell me about your illness," I said. My introduction had clued him into my profession, and as far as he was con-cerned, I was making a friendly follow-up visit to assess what he might need to stay at home and not proceed to hospice.

"Well, I've had cancer for years. It started about fifteen years ago and I have had operations in Arizona where we retired. We spend summers here to see our kids, but most of my time I live down there, so that's where most of this happened." He readily filled me in on the multiple surgeries, radiation and chemo treatments that had already been performed, but so disjointedly that I found myself thoroughly confused. "The doctors down there told me they wanted me to go back into the hospital in Arizona, but I told them, 'Nonsense! I'm going north to see my family.'"

"Did they say why they wanted you back in the hospital?" I asked.

"Well, they had this notion I am going to die. That doctor was full of gloom and doom and I wasn't going to take that. I told them my daughter is a nurse, and I was going where the medical care made sense."

"So what happened when you arrived...how long ago?" I looked to Charlotte for the answer.

"It's almost three weeks now. We got here, but only after a lot of difficulty. We had to stop often to let him rest. As soon as we arrived, we called Meredith right away." She spoke calmly, but her hands trembled in her lap. Nervously she looked toward Mario, whose lips were pinched in displeasure as his wife openly shared this information. His eyes narrowed as he shot her a look of rebuke and took back the conversation.

"Yes, and the next thing you know I was in the hospital again. Meredith had me see her doctor, and he said I was in bad shape, too. What's the matter with these doctors anyway? They're supposed to fix things, not see disaster everywhere."

Dodging the question, I asked, "What did they do in the hospital, Mario?"

"Oh, ran some tests. They said I was dehydrated and something about my chemistries were off." His off-handed remarks were blatant testimony to his steadfast determination not to take this seriously.

"And?" I let the question hang, waiting for him to fill in the blanks.

"They drew some fluid from my stomach. You know, it had blown up pretty big but now I'm back to how I used to be." The flippant bravado was designed to convince me all was just fine, but I noted him warily studying my reaction. His sidelong glance accentuated the yellow in his eyes, a stark contrast to his tanned and robust exterior.

You aren't fooling me. You're not quite as certain as you seem, I thought, but I decided not to react, knowing I would gain nothing by commenting.

"They wanted me to go over to this hospice unit. Do you know anything about that? You work in this business don't you? Is it any good? I mean, I can't just go some place and not know anything about it." The tumble of questions showed me he had far more concern than he was willing to convey, and his arms jerked in irritation as he thought about his situation.

"I know they gave you all kinds of information, Mario," I said to myself. "The hospice movement is one of the finest things we do in medicine, and there is no doubt in my mind they offered you excellent preparation. No use being impatient. Just teach him again."

I patiently told him about the hospice inpatient unit, what it would be like to be a patient there, what they could do to support him and make his days more comfortable.

"Your wife can go right with you and even stay all the time, if you prefer. That way you can still be together." Almost as an afterthought, I asked, "Why did they want you to go there?"

"They told me my cancer is too far gone to help and I can't go on living. But I am doing fine. They don't know what they are talking about." Mario returned to his favorite doctor theme.

Clearly arguing with the persuasive Mario wasn't going to work. "Just see what information you can get, Joy. You can form a plan later," I reminded myself. I switched the talk to health care proxies, living wills, do not resuscitate orders, and found that Mario had none of these.

"If you go into a coma and stop breathing, how do you feel about being resuscitated and kept alive on a breathing machine?" I asked. "Especially if it meant you would still remain in a coma and couldn't be better again?"

"Oh, I would never want that!" exploded Mario, raising his determined chin higher; his jaw set even tighter. A flash of anger blazed in his eyes, and it was clear his resistance was building to admitting anything was wrong. I chose to back off, knowing I couldn't be an ally if I confronted him and lost. Not wanting to face what he had so far successfully dodged, Mario changed the subject.

We talked about his trip from Arizona, his family, and trivial matters, until eventually Mario wandered back into the topic at hand. "I'm not just certain what I should do next. What do you think, Joy?"

"I think you can trust your doctor. He is a fine physician and will do all he can to help you sort this out. Do you mind if I talk to Meredith, and maybe we can figure out a plan?" I tried to be casual.

"Would you? I think that would be great. You two just put your heads together and see what you can cook up. Maybe then I'll get some sense out of all this." Mario rubbed his hands together, looking happier, as he grasped at the chance to be back in control. We wrapped up the conversation after I checked his vital signs, listened to his heart and lungs, and generally assessed his condition, which was shaky at best. I promised to come back the next day, after consulting with Meredith.

Late that afternoon I called Meredith to introduce myself and update her on my visit. "I'm so glad there's someone to help me sort this out. As far as I can see my father has ignored all the warning signals that things aren't getting any better. He just plows on denying that cancer is going to make any difference in his life."

"It's a wonder he managed to drive here without an accident," I marveled.

"Isn't it? I worry so much about my mother. She's no match for his strong will. Wouldn't you know, he refused to go to hospice and is giving my mother a hard time, not listening to anything she says, follow the medical advice, or even take the medicines they have prescribed. This may sound terrible, but he has been so difficult, if it weren't for my mother, I don't think I would choose to cope with him either."

"That has to be tough, Meredith."

"No kidding. That's my father, stubborn to the core. But, for my mother's sake I do all I can. My mom's a really wonderful person who has endured way too much. This time, I don't know how to help her. Did he listen to you?"

"Meredith, I see what you mean. He runs a tight offensive strategy! But he didn't throw me out. Maybe because I worked at charming him, and so far, I haven't suggested anything controversial."

"That's good news. I mean, about not getting thrown out. If I suggest anything he doesn't want to hear, he not only is nasty with me, but he gets mad and takes it out on my mother, yelling at her and blaming her for anything he can think of. My mother isn't young herself any more. I can't see how she deals with all this, and I'm anxious to prevent an emergency that will leave her any more spent then she already is. Right at the moment she just sits and shakes and prays." Meredith expelled an audible long slow breath of frustration, and then went on in a strained voice. "Do you think there's any hope you, we, whoever, can get him to go into the hospice unit?"

"I don't know. All we can do is give it our best try, Meredith. Unless your father has been to a lawyer I don't know about, he's in terrible shape legally. There is no health care proxy. He says he doesn't want resuscitation, but he's done nothing legal to say so in a way that will be observed. Your mother doesn't even have a piece of paper permitting her to speak for him if he goes into a coma and can't tell us himself what he wants."

"Joy, if you try to get him to make my mother a health care proxy, he'll balk all the more. He has been so difficult for her! The car isn't even in her name. He just keeps accusing her of wanting to see him dead, so she can have all his money. As if my mom ever had a devious thought in her life. Don't get me wrong, Joy. I love my father as my father, but with what he has put my mother and everyone through I am only in on this for what I can do to ease my mother's life. Making her the health care proxy isn't going to be it." Meredith's voice tightened in desperation, her words punctuated with anger as she let out her frustration. I was certain it had been a lifetime of one frustration after another.

"Would you be willing to be his health care proxy, if I can talk him into signing for you to be appointed? I'll go back to the apartment with you in the morning and try, if you are willing to assume the responsibility."

"Do you really think that will work?" She sounded dubious.

"We'll never know unless we try. He gives me the feeling he's much more concerned than he lets on. I wouldn't be surprised if he's quaking in his boots." I related the subtle signs Mario had given, as he cagily studied my reaction to his flat pronouncements that everything was in good shape. "That told me he knew all was not as well as he'd have me believe, and his jaundiced eyes tell me it's only a matter of time before his problems escalate."

"For my mother's sake, I will consent to be the one he appoints as his proxy. But don't be surprised if it doesn't work! I know how stormy and impossible my father can be. He may dig in his heels and say no."

"The worst that can happen is he'll throw me out. I'm a big girl and can survive that, so try not to sweat it, Meredith," I reassured her. She made arrangements to meet me the next morning and let me into the locked-entry apartment building.

I hung up the phone and sat staring at the receiver with an uneasy feeling in the pit of my stomach. "Better suspend all preconceived notions or you will create the very scenario you have imagined," I said to myself. "After all, until you try this approach, he is entitled to no previous conclusions from his nurse about what will or can be done. He may be just about the most formidable man you've ever seen, but he's also very ill. Sooner or later that's going to settle the battle."

The sun was sending its optimistic warmth our way as we met in the morning. Meredith was waiting for me as arranged, her pleasant smile framed by dark curly hair. I shook her hand in introduction, the icy cold grip a stark contrast from her assured and relaxed appearance.

Our strategy was quickly reviewed during the rickety ascent in the ancient elevator, creaking and groaning its way to the third floor. "Don't say anything, Meredith. I'll do the talking, and then, if he is to be angry, we can always shift all of the blame for this to me. After all, he doesn't ever have to see me again, and that way it won't be worse for you. If he explodes at me, you can always claim temporary insanity for thinking I was a friend and be properly horrified, or whatever else is necessary to maintain your position."

"My position. Yeah. Some position. He doesn't even listen to me." Her dejected face said it all.

"I'll give it my best shot," I said, as I touched her arm. Tucking my folder under my arm I stepped out into the dark and dreary hallway that matched Meredith's mood. I hoped I would get to use the papers I had brought in case we could get him to sign a health care proxy.

"Just don't mention my mom. He'll really balk if you do," she cautioned.

Pausing for a moment I silently offered up a little prayer. "Dear God. I don't know how we are doing this, but Charlotte has suffered enough. Give me the words, and I'll try to do my part and get me out of your way. I sure don't know what we are going to say, but here goes."

A very different Mario greeted us. Ashen faced and clearly yellow all over, the dramatic change since yesterday was a startling reminder of just how ill he was. Before my hand left the doorknob Mario was on his feet, looking angry, as he demanded, "Joy, am I going to die?"

I took a deep breath. I have a steadfast policy not to lie to patients. Hospice nurses know people have a sacred need to know the truth so they can finish their unfinished business and put their affairs in order. Lying does not help. Meeting his insistent gaze with my own steady one I looked into his eyes and said simply, "Yes, Mario. You are."

"Well, why hasn't anyone told me?" he blustered. "I'm the last to find out."

"They have told you. You are the one who told me so yesterday. You just have such a strong positive outlook, you didn't hear your own words." Mario sat down abruptly, the wind taken out of his sails by the realization of what had come from his own mouth.

I continued, "The best estimate we have, Mario, is that soon your liver may shut down. If, and when that happens, you will most likely go into a coma from liver failure. It may be a few days or even a couple of weeks. The tests you had indicate it is not very far away."

"Well, I've got to make plans! Someone should have told me!" Mario began to sputter. The panicky look in his eyes and pulsing muscle in his jaw signaled his fear.

Not glancing at Meredith or her mother, who were sitting quietly with an arm around each other, I decided to take the proverbial bull by the horns. "I'm telling you now, Mario. You seem to me like a man who has always run a tight ship and stayed in control."

"You bet I have! You can't leave things to others. They might let you down!" Mario gained strength as he returned to the prominent belief ruling his life.

"Well, Mario. If you go into coma right now, you don't have anything spelled out about the way you want things done. That's not typical of you. Do you realize, as it is now, you could be put on a breathing machine, even though you don't want one? Even without your choice, because you wouldn't be able to say no? Do you realize what terrible shape your paperwork is in, if you want to stay in charge of your own life?" I paused and saw my words had found their mark.

"Furthermore, I'll bet you don't even know what could happen, if you were on a respirator or went into a coma. You'd have no control over anything. You wouldn't know what was happening or have say over any of it." I kept my eyes locked with his, giving him my full attention as if there were no others in the room.

Mario was at a total loss for words. His hand trembled as he raised it to rub his forehead in silent perplexity.

"Fortunately, there is a way you can be in coma and still be in perfect charge of what is happening. There is only one way for you to remain in control, but there is a way to do so." He sat forward, his fearful eyes now brightening with curiosity.

"You can sign a health care proxy, and the person you appoint will absolutely carry out your wishes. You have a daughter who is a nurse and she will know exactly what you want. If you appoint her, she'll carry out your every wish. Just think, you might not be able to talk, but you'll still be in charge of every detail. She will know exactly what you would want done and do it. It means you will still be calling all the shots, and have it exactly the way you want it. That's absolutely the only way you can do this and stay in control."

"Who's going to take care of me? She can't do this. I'm a big man and she's very little." He motioned in the direction of his silent wife, sitting patiently with her daughter.

"We have a hospice unit where you can go, and there are nurses and attendants on duty around the clock. They will do things to help you as you wish. Charlotte can be there to help you as she always has. Do you want to be on a breathing machine, if you stop breathing?" I asked.

"Hell, no! No way I'm going to be on a machine," he roared.

"Well, I have the correct paper to state your wishes right here, and if you want, you can sign it. Then Meredith can go right over to the doctor's office, and we can make arrangements for you to go into the hospice unit this very day. That way, if you go into a coma, the staff will know exactly how you want things, and your daughter will absolutely see your wishes are carried out the way you want them. You will be the one who made the decision, just like you have all your life. It's the only way for you to stay in command of your wishes." I pushed the paper in Mario's direction. He took it in his hand, studying the words intently.

Glancing now at his daughter he asked gruffly, "You willing to do this for me, my way?"

"Daddy, I'll do whatever you ask me to, just like you tell me you want it." Meredith gave extra emphasis to the words, her face intent and serious as she gave her father her word.

"Give me a pen, Joy. I want things to be done right." He reached for the paper and pen, unable to resist staying in charge, even if fate dealt him a coma. Decisively he wrote "Do Not Resuscitate," appointed Meredith to be in charge in the event he could not, and signed his name.

"Mario, it's good to see someone who knows what they want and can say so. We will do everything we can to help you as you wish. That is the hospice philosophy, to support people in their own choices and honor their wishes." I answered the questions Mario asked. Gradually he lost all his bluster, as he was firmly back in the driver's seat, giving directions on how to get him to the hospice inpatient unit.

We needed to wrap up the visit before Mario changed his mind. "Meredith can go right now to the doctor, get the papers signed the way you have chosen, make arrangements, and you can go into the unit today. I'll stop up and see you in a few days. Good luck!" Mario thanked me, and shook my hand, his yellowed face grave and drawn.

At the elevator, Meredith and I talked quickly. "I don't believe you got him to sign that! Joy, I'm in shock. I told my mother, 'Don't say anything. Let's see what she can do,' and we sat down."

"You're not the only one amazed. You need to get to the doctor pronto, and bring this about before he has second thoughts about going into the unit."

"I'm on my way."

On my descent to the street, the elevator creaked and groaned, sounding as if it were on its final journey. I found my way to my car and sat behind the steering wheel, squinting in the bright sunlight that once more commanded the day. "I'm stunned. In my whole life I've never promised someone a coma. It just seems like decisive language was the only talk he understands." I spent a few minutes going over the conversation in my mind, too numbed by the drama that had unfolded to trust myself to drive. "So much for your desire to be gentle and supportive," I told myself. "It just clashed head on with his need to see the truth whatever way he would."

Later that evening I called Meredith. "It went well and my dad is in the hospice unit. Mom will be with him. I still almost can't believe it. He just couldn't resist staying in charge. How did you know what to say?"

"Darned if I know, but it suddenly occurred to me that what really happens, when you sign the legal safeguards available, is that you remain in control. To tell you the truth, Merry, I think the guys upstairs just guided me. How did it go after I left? I would have given a lot to be a fly on the wall."

"I went right off to the doctor and got the papers signed. By the time I came back, he was changing his mind. He started to return to the doctors-don't-know-anything theme he's counted on for so long. I told him he could come home again if he found the doctors were wrong, and I bustled him off before he thought up any more arguments. He must be losing his strength that he backed down enough to get this far."

Meredith shared details of the admission to the hospice inpatient unit and how her parents had been very pleased with what they saw. Her voice turned wistful as she recounted their day. "I just hope, for my mom's sake, that he will back off from her for a bit and give her a break. Usually when others are around he is very charming, and he really turned it on for the staff. He won't be able to keep it up indefinitely, and sooner or later who he is will pop out."

"Anyway, if it doesn't last, Mom has some help dealing with him now. She's exhausted. Can you imagine driving up here with him like he insisted? She knew he wasn't well, but he wasn't going to listen to anyone. It's a miracle they weren't both killed!" Stress laced her words once more.

"Meredith, the atmosphere in hospice units is the closest thing to unconditional love I've ever seen. If there ever is a chance to grow, it is there, where everyone accepts you just as you are and gives you the maximum choice. It will be fascinating to see what that brings to your dad's life. There your mom will have emotional support too, and she may be able to heal the hurt from all this in a way that exceeds your expectations. I know you are very worried about her. Try to let yourself relax a little about her care. Meanwhile, don't forget who carried out this assignment. You deserve a real pat on the back for braving your father's anger one more time."

It was several days before my schedule allowed me to visit the inpatient unit. Just walking into the tastefully decorated area that felt more like a friendly high quality hotel than a place to die lifted my spirits. I rounded the corner with its pale yellow embossed wallpaper and stepped into the office. "How's it going for Mario?" I asked one of the nurses.

"Let me tell you what happened." Beth's face shone with excitement as she looked up from the desk to talk with me. "Charlotte sits and prays for him, in between waiting on him for any need he has. He was very charming for several days, but he couldn't hide forever. He would flare at her for no good reason. He can be so nasty and caustic. We just try to be present and give support to them both. But yesterday, as Charlotte sat there and said the rosary for him, he reached over and took her hand. Out of the blue he must have said something really important. And now Charlotte is a different woman. So much more peaceful."

"Why? What did she do?" I asked.

"I'm not exactly sure what happened, but she cried non stop for two hours. Charlotte kept saying she never thought she would hear those words, even though she's prayed for this for years."

He reached out to her in a caring way. What wonderful growth for Mario, I thought.

Walking into his room, I said nothing of the incident, but as I looked at Charlotte the transformation was obvious. Gone was the droop in her posture. In its place was a serenity I never thought I would see. My heart swelled with compassion as I thought about the trials she had endured before reaching this point. Mario was napping, and I drew her out into the hall.

"Charlotte, something is so changed for you. May I ask what happened?"

"Joy, I never thought I'd live to hear those words. Do you know, he just suddenly reached over and took my hand and said, 'You're the best thing that's ever happened to me. I've been awful to you and I'm so sorry. I love you.'" Her eyes shone with the tears that spilled over yet one more time, and her hand clasped mine and squeezed it tightly, unable to go on.

Silently we embraced, the quietly sobbing Charlotte encircled by my speechless hug. "Miracles do happen, Charlotte." I whispered in her ear, as my tears spilled over into hers.

Meredith phoned to update me. "You wouldn't believe how it came about, Joy. My father has been getting weaker, and just the night before, he put his arms up toward heaven and begged, 'Please, dear God. Take me home.' Well, he felt he got back a message, 'Not before you clean up your act.' He became very quiet after that. My mom just went on praying for him, never missing a beat.

"Then today, while my mother said the rosary for him, he reached over and took her hand and told her, 'I've been terrible to you. And I'm so sorry. You're the best thing that ever happened to me. I know I've been taking things out on you and been so unfair. I love you very much, and I want you to know that.' She cried for hours with joy, that he had seen the truth. All those years she never gave up trying to reach him. She is so much more at peace! Joy, I am so glad for my mother. It's wonderful to see what has happened, and even if he doesn't make amends with anyone else, seeing my mother reprieved after all these years is a blessing."

I smiled into the phone, the moment alive with wonderful poignancy.

She shared more about his stay on the hospice unit. "There's a nun who is a nurse and she talks to him just like you," she said. "Remember how you wondered about that? Well, that works with him every time. She just shoots straight from the hip, like you did, and it seems to be the language he understands best."

A little more than a week passed, and I never got back to visit Mario, or to visit with Meredith. Our answering machines talked to each other in my absence. Before I could visit again Meredith left a message on my machine. "Dad died this afternoon and I wanted you to know."

Where does the time go, and how do we get so busy we can't work in visiting more? I said to myself. "I am so thankful Meredith had help going through his death. No matter how I work at it I can't be everywhere at once. No good preaching to others that guilt sets you up for punishment if you aren't going to practice letting it go yourself, Joy."

As I drove to the funeral parlor two days later it was another glorious day, filled with sunshine and promise, but my mind whirled with worry about Meredith. Grief is so often more complicated if there are regrets. Feeling protective of this brave and tenacious daughter, I wondered how to help her with the feelings I feared would be present from losing a father with whom she never had an opportunity to set things straight. Controlling my concern, I entered the funeral home, determined to be there for her, no matter how she was dealing with her loss.

Charlotte caught my eye first. Smiling and gracious, all shyness now evaporated, she floated among the friends and family who had come to pay their respects. Her relaxed and peaceful demeanor told me that her inner serenity had endured and flourished. A momentary flash of joy swept away my concern, as I remembered the tiny, frail lady I had originally met. There it is to see, I thought. The wonderful power of forgiveness; it can change the lives of all involved for the rest of their days.

Meredith sat composed in a chair at the side of the room. Seeing me, she sprung out of her chair and bounced over to see me, her face radiant and peaceful. "Oh, Joy. I can't wait to tell you what happened." She hugged me tightly, reluctant to let the moment go, and then drew me by the hand to sit in a chair beside her.

"Remember when my father asked for my mother's forgiveness? Well, after that, one by one, he talked to each of my brothers and said, 'I'm so sorry for the way I have been to you' and asked for their forgiveness. Just as he asked Mom. He talked to everyone. All except me. Now, I was very happy for my family. It made me feel joy for them, because I've never felt I was the only one who suffered from his attitudes and behavior. I know we all experienced his outbursts. But it really hurt that he wasn't saying anything to me."

I had no difficulty understanding how much that hurt. I managed a small compassionate smile, and nodded.

"I even talked to the Sister, when she was on duty. I told her, 'Apparently I am not going to have that experience to ease my pain.' She told me, 'Perhaps you have to ask for his forgiveness first.' That made me so angry! 'Ask for his forgiveness?' I asked her. 'I haven't done anything. I've covered for him for years, over and over, as he did and said things that were awful. I don't have anything to ask forgiveness for!'" She paused, remembering, and then went on.

"Things progressed, with my father getting weaker and weaker. He just couldn't seem to die. I kept going up to see him, taking care of him anyway I could. My mother stayed at his side, peaceful. I was so happy for her! But I felt really hurt that Dad had not said anything to me." Meredith fumbled with her ring, eyes focused far away, remembering, and I wondered how to help her.

"Finally, his eyes became very dry and painful, because they were not closing completely anymore. I put eye drops into one eye, and he flinched from the pain. I said, 'Oh, Daddy! I'm so sorry that hurt you. I didn't mean to hurt you!' After all, I'm not heartless you know. It's just…there were so many years of pain. Then I put drops into the other eye, and he flinched again. I could see it really hurt. Again I said, 'Oh, Daddy! I am so sorry to hurt you.' And then he said, 'No, I'm sorry. I've hurt you, and I am so sorry.'

"Joy, I couldn't even move. I was riveted to the spot and couldn't get a single word to come out of my mouth. I went on taking care of him a little bit more and then I leaned over and said into his ear, 'You're forgiven, Daddy.' Do you know what, Joy? He died one hour later."

Meredith's joyous face said it all. Watching as she and her mother greeted visitors and attended to the details of the calling hours, I could see the transformation. They are

glowing. I don't think I've ever seen people glow at a funeral parlor before. How amazing! I thought.

As I prepared to leave, Meredith excused herself and
slipped over to say good-bye to me, gracious and smiling,
the transformation from pain to peace apparent to all who
saw her face. "How will I ever thank you, Joy? I can never
say enough to let you know how much I appreciate your
help."

"You don't need to thank me, Meredith. Thank yourself
and your mom for never giving up hope. Thank the wonderful guidance that is there for all of us, if we remember to
ask. When some time has passed, and you have given yourself time to grieve, consider becoming a hospice volunteer
to help others. You just passed a crash course in what it is all
about and will have everything to offer others. That is the
only thanks we ever need; each one helping another and
then a beautiful chain is created wherein the helping hands
never stop."

I drove out of the parking lot and felt an incredible sense
of satisfaction for the quantum leap that I had just witnessed. Such significant changes! It was almost too much to
grasp. Smiling to myself, I said another little prayer to my
helpers upstairs. "Thank you for all the help. I didn't know
how we were going to do it. Well, I don't kid myself who
did this, and I thank you. More than I can ever say."

Celebration

The value of life does not lie in the number of years but in the use you make of them.

~ Michel de Montaigne

For a moment when I pulled into the driveway I had a flash of deja vu. I thought, This is the same apartment building where I came for another patient last year. How strange. I felt the jolt of that realization, as I parked my car and headed for the back door.

Donna opened the door herself, and I knew, in an instant, this was the right place. Her slow measured gait, emaciated and pale appearance, and large eyes that were way too big for her face, told me she was acutely ill. There is something about so much weight loss that makes the eyes appear bigger than usual. What a tell tale sign, I thought.

She invited me into the living room where she could lie down while I checked on her condition. Another nurse from my agency had opened her case to homecare two days earlier, and I was doing a follow up visit to assess her needs and become acquainted.

"My paper work says you are fifty-two years old?" I asked. She nodded solemnly. "And you have five adult children?" Again she nodded, this time with a smile breaking over her face. "I'm impressed, Donna. You don't look old enough to have grown up kids and grandchildren."

Donna giggled and shot back, "Well, I am. I got an early start." She smiled and looked down a bit shyly. We continued to converse, initiating the rapport that is so important between nurse and patient.

Later I would come to see Donna's basic reticence was balanced with a ready little giggle that was almost a trademark for her. It would show me the humor she brought to life and was an attempt to cover her basically timid nature. But that first day it startled me to hear her laugh so mischievously, such a sharp contrast to her seriously ill condition. "Even now, when obviously she is very ill," I said to myself, "she can see the humor. That tells me a lot about the spirit of this gentle woman." The giggle added to her youthful look—which somehow overrode her weak and emaciated condition—and was in stark contrast to her highly fragile state. It was hard to believe she was a grandmother.

"How's it going?" I switched to the business at hand.

"Not too well," she replied, with her large doleful eyes fixed upon me. Quietly she studied me. I noticed her look was suddenly sad.

"Translate for me exactly what that means," I coaxed. I knew from years of experience that nice people don't feel free to complain. I smiled at her and waited for her answer.

"It's this nausea." Donna explained as she patted her stomach gingerly.

Slowly I began examining her regimen, searching for understanding of just where she was in the progression of her disease. Reviewing all of her medications, I discovered one she wasn't taking correctly. "That could be the culprit as it directly affects digestion. Let me write out a schedule for you, Donna. It's devilishly hard to keep track of the ball game when you feel rotten. You feel really awful, or just kind of punk?" I hoped my non-medical terminology would help her feel easier about complaining.

"Pretty awful," she said. Her large eyes widened and she slowly nodded her head. Her voice, however, remained even and calm, with no trace of irritation for the severe symptom she was reporting.

I drew her out, sensing how difficult it is to make conversation when you feel "pretty awful." Donna talked of her frustration at never feeling well, her even-keeled voice in stark contrast to the overwhelming irritation persistent nausea was causing in her life. Eventually I felt we knew each other well enough I could tentatively take her hand.

Holding it lightly in mine, I said, "Donna, you and I will need to work together to solve this and other problems that arise. I sense you are a really nice person used to putting up with things and not complaining. I need for you to feel free to tell me everything and know that I don't see that as complaining, just communicating. That is how I can best help you." Donna's relieved smile and nod told me she was comfortable with our arrangement. I finished reviewing and adjusting her entire regimen to control her symptoms and prepared to leave.

"I'll be back in two days, to check on the effectiveness of your medicine once you're taking it correctly," I reassured her. With a smile and a friendly wave I said good-bye.

I wondered if I had reached her. So many people who have cancer are such nice people. Too nice! They just suffer in silence. What will it take to teach her to speak up so she can have at least a little peace? I thought.

Gradually over the next few weeks I learned more about Donna. She had married at a young age, raised five children, choosing to stay home to do so. When her marriage dissolved, she returned to school to become more marketable in the work force. She had found a fulfilling job after completing some courses to update her skills. Now, after working for a couple of years, she found she had cancer that was diagnosed in a fairly advanced state. "I thought the hard times were finally behind me, but I guess I was wrong." Donna kept a tight rein on her facial expression as she talked about this realization that so affected her future.

I let my face register the disappointment I felt for her, and wondered how much her characteristic putting aside of her self had contributed to failing to notice symptoms earlier. I doubted Donna really knew how to place herself as a priority. On the other hand, some illnesses remain relatively symptom free until it's too late. "Looks like Donna is one of those. How I hate to see this is someone so young," I said to myself.

Statistics indicated cancer patients do better when they are a little more crusty and able to be outspoken. After years of seeing how many really nice people have cancer, I am inclined to believe the statistics. Better to be able to say some version of "I don't like that" than to bury it within, where it could come back to affect one later. No wonder the research finds a curmudgeon personality may have a better change for recovery, I thought. Clearly there is no curmudgeon in this household!

The next few weeks were a battle to get Donna to talk about her feelings, for life-long patterns are hard to break, even with a nurse prodding you. "I need to know how you are feeling in order to help. The squeaky wheel gets the grease, you know. I've got to find some way to make you into a squeaky wheel."

"Not much change," Donna said. She continued to find complaining totally alien to her nature. Little by little we found our way, as together we battled her fairly advanced liver cancer and the symptoms of nausea and extreme fatigue she experienced. We became a team, and I became more adept at figuring out what was bothering her.

It soon became clear the course of Donna's illness included frequent ups and downs. Days of feeling "pretty awful," during which we adjusted medications until we found relief, were followed by a day or two, all the way up to a few in a row, of good days. Try as we might, we couldn't make that pattern extend before she experienced some more down time. Never being able to count on how she felt slowly took its toll. Her ability to function was eeking away bit by bit, right along with my belief we were going to find quality time for this tender, fragile woman.

"I think we'd better put some more aide service hours in here. You finding it harder to do even just the basic care you need?"

She nodded. "I didn't want to complain, Joy."

She never would have asked. I am so thankful I'm reading her more accurately, I thought.

The continued return to feeling "pretty awful" more than blocked any effort Donna made to make each day count. As a practical measure I poured out medications for a whole week at a time, so she couldn't inadvertently forget a dosage. Meanwhile it felt like we were on a roller coaster with no chance to adjust before the direction changed once more.

Donna had a very close relationship with her only daughter, who happened to work in a business just a few blocks away. The proximity of her job allowed Janeen to visit her mother freely, and she took full advantage of the opportunity. I knew her frequent visits did much to keep her mother's days from unrelieved boredom. All of her children were regular visitors, and I felt admiration for the success Donna had achieved raising her children, in spite of her difficult times.

On the whole, Donna began to smile more, and managed to move forward in spite of her disease, and in spite of her carefully struck balance to remain somewhere between mature insight and unexpressed sadness. We managed to get out some of the disappointments, a few of the worries and an occasional regret. Always, when we talked about her family, she instantly perked up.

"I have five grandchildren," she would say, beaming with pride. In those moments, Donna stopped looking worn and ill. The glow of happiness filled her face in a way all the nutritional supplements and medications had failed to do. "You should hear what's happened now," she would say, as she told me stories about them, beaming happily. The joy took over her face, making her look even younger.

Or I would ask, "What's new on the kid front?" We managed to have a few fairly comfortable weeks, with Donna emerging from her reserved manner to be a proud and beaming grandmother, temporarily insulated from the nagging reality that was her usual day.

So it came as a surprise to arrive one day and find her clearly depressed. Characteristically, she offered little about why, as she answered me with small monosyllables and averted her eyes from mine. I went on a fishing expedition to see if I could unearth anything.

"Let me see. I guess I'm going to have to figure this out. You by any chance feeling discouraged about your lack of progress?" She nodded. "And you're worried because you aren't as strong as you were just a little while ago."

"Yes, it doesn't seem fair." She melted back into the pillows of the couch, rather like a blown up doll that just lost its air.

"What part feels the most unfair?"

She gave a small shrug. No words came forward to explain this sad, hard moment.

Suddenly I had a hunch. "Donna, is there some event you are trying to make it through to see?

"My son's wedding," she replied in a barely audible tone.

"Your son is getting married? When?"

"In two and a half weeks."

"And you don't think you're going to be strong enough to make it, right?" I was staring at her now and she nodded her head, utterly dejected.

"Why didn't you tell me before? That's important."

"He just graduated from college in May after he worked his way through school. I was too sick to go to the graduation ceremony. I didn't think I would have to miss the wedding, too." For once Donna let her emotions show, as she stared at the floor, shoulders slumped in defeat. Without a word she reached up to her cheek and brushed away the tears streaming down her face.

"Donna, listen. Maybe you don't have to miss the wedding. You know, there are some things we can try, to buy a little time and increase your strength. Let me talk with your doctor and see what we can figure out. I took a patient to a wedding once and she did great. What we did was set up a cot at the reception where she could have a rest when she needed it and that worked out really well. I'd be only too happy to help you do the same. Don't give up yet. Let's see what we can figure out." Donna looked up, nodded slightly, willing to briefly suspend her desolation and give me a change to intervene.

"How fast the picture can change!" I told myself. "I'm so glad I found out in time, and that she trusts me. Now to see what we can do."

The next few days were a flurry of phone calls to problem solve and check possibilities. I called her doctor and arranged for Donna to visit with him, had blood chemistries drawn, checked with the restaurant where the reception was to be held to be certain I could set up a cot in one of their offices, and called the volunteer office to make the necessary arrangements.

"Your doctor is clearly in our camp and is as determined as we are to get you to this wedding. We're going to think positively here, and order the wheelchair. It's portable and you should have it on hand anyway, for keeping your visits to the doctor," I told her.

"Whatever you think." The words were brief, but she allowed herself to hold back the waves of defeat and discouragement that came in such unwelcome bursts, knowing she was powerless to fix this for herself. She did the one thing open to her. Donna suspended her disbelief and let her nurse attempt to bring about an act of hope she had all but given up for lost. Sneaking a peek at her, I saw she was pleased at my efforts to achieve our goal, and for a brief moment the tide of inevitability was held at bay.

I called the equipment center at my agency and ordered the wheelchair. "And Mike, make it a really nice one. This one's going to a wedding, her son's, and it's really important."

"Okay. I'll see what I can do."

The blood chemistry reports came back and the news

was not good. Her values were unbalanced from all the nausea and vomiting she had experienced. We arranged to have her go to the hospital to receive intravenous fluids for a few hours and then return home. She was bound to feel some improvement with her chemistries corrected, but she needed close supervision while receiving the fluids. "We need to be certain she doesn't go into heart failure," her doctor had instructed. Donna did well with the procedure but only felt a little improved. I placed another call to the doctor requesting a call back as soon as possible.

Donna's spirits seemed to have perked up a notch in spite of the unresolved nausea. "To what do we attribute this cheery manner, Donna?" I asked.

Her face lit up, eyes sparkling, and with a little giggle said, "Look in the corner."

I swung around to follow her gaze, and there, sitting in the corner, was a brand new, shiny, black and chrome wheelchair. "Isn't is great?" Donna asked.

"Wow! You're going to ride down the aisle in a shiny new set of wheels. Very impressive. You have quite a chariot waiting for you." We joked and laughed, but clearly the wheelchair had brought something to Donna's day we had otherwise been unable to achieve.

Privately, I called Mike and said, "You are a doll! Donna couldn't be happier if we were sending her to the wedding in a chauffeured limousine. Thanks, Mike."

I could almost hear Mike blushing at the other end of the line. "It was nothing. Glad to do it for her."

Meanwhile, we needed to make the other arrangements. "Anyone in the family got a camp cot we can borrow?" I asked Donna. She agreed to ask around. Together we planned with the home health aide which sheets, pillows and cases we would take to the reception, making lists as we thought of fresh ideas. "You have them all ready for me on that day, and I'll get them over to the reception and set everything up. Better have a lightweight cover, too. It may be summer, but lying around in air conditioning is bound to cool you down."

"Already have one picked out." She giggled.

"Oh, I keep forgetting to ask. Do you have a camera? You're going to want pictures of all this."

Donna nodded happily, and added the camera and film to the list.

I had placed phone calls to our volunteer department, during my flurry of arrangements, to ask for a camp cot and one or two volunteers who would accompany Donna to the wedding and reception. "I'll have everything set up and emergency supplies ready. I'll even write out instructions and meet them there if that will help."

"I'll look into it right away," she said. "Sounds like an important moment and we'll do our best to find someone."

The doctor phoned back. He would be willing to repeat the intravenous fluids in a week and see if we could achieve a cumulative effect to increase Donna's strength. "Can't we do something about this non-stop nausea for a few days before and during the wedding? Seems like she's entitled to a reprieve, for such an important event."

The doctor reviewed her complete medication schedule while I waited, less than confident there was a solution. "How about that horribly expensive drug they've just developed?" I asked. "Can we try it for her?"

"I would be willing to put her on an extremely potent anti-nausea medication for seventy-two hours to try and control the nausea, so she can eat something at the reception, and give her a third time with intravenous fluids the day before the wedding. I don't think her system can handle much more than that though."

With a sigh of relief, I realized I had been holding my breath.

"Donna, this is great!" I told her as I hung up the phone. "You have a very understanding doctor who just handed us a solution. We can start the pills two days before the wedding and take the medicine all the day and evening of the wedding. I just know you'll be fine."

"Okay. Whatever you say." She agreed, smiling serenely at last.

With hope renewed and such vigorous efforts being made to solve the problems, Donna perked up another notch. By anyone's standards she was not well, but I knew how determination and excitement carry one through otherwise daunting situations. I was betting on her love of family overriding all the obstacles from her rapidly declining health. If we just provided the support so she didn't feel like a burden to her family, almost all of whom were in the wedding party, she was bound to do well.

The volunteer office called me back. "We feel terrible but we haven't been able to come up with either a cot or a volunteer. All our volunteers who would love to do this happen to be out of town on vacation. We've called everybody we can possibly think of with no luck. I hate to let you down, but it's summertime and that weekend is a prime vacation time. What are you going to do?"

My heart sank, with the unexpected assault of her words. "Don't know just yet. But we'll figure out something. We just have to. This is a once in a life time event." I hung up the phone, my mind in a whirl. "This just can't be happening!" I

fretted to myself. "Going to this wedding is all that's keeping
Donna hopeful in spite of her miserable symptoms. We've got
to do this somehow! I can't imagine missing your child's
wedding."

She wilted before my eyes, the wind taken from her sails
as she contemplated the bad news. I told her, "There's a way
to solve this. We just have to be smart enough to figure it
out." She gamely hung in there, at my request, and took the
long view.

To keep her spirits up, we focused on the new outfit she
had purchased with her daughter a few weeks earlier. They
had shopped for the wedding while Donna still had the
strength to do so. Now she showed it to me. "You've never
seen me all dressed up." She giggled as she allowed herself a
sideways glance in my direction. "I'm always in shorts, slacks
or pajamas." I noticed the sparkle back in her eyes and felt a
momentary sense of relief. To know that with her limited
energy, and the reality we didn't have help for her to go to
the wedding, she felt determined to focus on dressing up for
the occasion validated how important this event was to her.
It also said volumes about Donna's ability to hang in there
and be positive, and that increased my determination to
solve our problem.

"Donna, it's gorgeous. You're going to look great." I gave
her a hug and hoped I was successfully covering my mount-
ing concern over our situation. I was, in fact, approaching
panic that my best efforts had come up empty.

I sought a solution at our weekly patient conference,
where staff discussed cases and problem solved together,
knowing many heads are better than one. "I'd like to be
given permission to be her volunteer and take her to the
wedding reception. I did this once before, years ago, with a

patient who was dying. So I have a clear idea how to proceed, and don't have any fear about it working out well.
Who would be a more logical choice? I know by looking at
her how she feels, and just what's worked and hasn't, since
she's my patient."

"I'd like to think you could go home from your job and
leave it. That's what we have a volunteer department for."
The curt statement came from one of the department heads,
and resembled being struck in the face with a wet wash-
cloth. Hasn't she been listening? I thought. What does she
think we have been trying to do?

"The volunteer department isn't able to solve this one.
This isn't about me being unable to leave my job. This is
about a woman who is about to die, who's looking at missing her son's wedding. That almost certainly means she will
not die in peace. I am willing to be her volunteer. Why not
let me this once? I've never asked before."

The group skirted around the issue and moved onto
other matters with no clear decision. My heart sank. Not
one person spoke up in recognition of Donna's need to get
to this all-important wedding. Perhaps no one wanted to
cross an authority figure, once she had spoken so blatantly.
Ignoring the decision left me unsettled, but it did nothing
to alter my determination.

As for the cot, I knew where there was one forty miles
away at my summer camp, so that night I just hopped into
my car and retrieved it. "One down and one to go," I told
Donna. "Next thing is to solve the volunteer situation."

"Look," I found myself saying to my supervisor. "I know
and understand all the reasons nurses on a case aren't supposed to be over involved. It's not that I can't leave my
work. It's that I've done this before, and I know how well it

can work out. There isn't a volunteer available who feels they can handle this request. If there were, I would have no problem turning this over to them. Besides, I know this patient very well, so I would make the perfect volunteer. I can just look at her and know how she's feeling. Couldn't we please stretch the rules and let me be her volunteer this one time?" I paused and looked into the face of my supervisor, hoping to gauge her response. "I'd be willing to sign off legally on liability or whatever you ask."

"The only liability would be if you drove. Are you planning to drive her in a car?" she asked.

"No, I don't have to do that. Her family can easily manage that. Besides, what's the difference if I volunteer someplace else or do my time here? I'm a volunteer in life, and it makes sense for me to be the one who handles the situation this time."

She hesitated, looking down at her desk, and then said, "Go ahead. And one thing more, Joy." She looked up at me and I felt a pang of anxiety as I wondered what was coming. "Have a good time."

I felt a tumble of relief, triumph, excitement, gratitude, and a feeling of winning at last rushing through my otherwise frustrating day. Resisting the urge to give her a bear hug, I thanked her and hurried off to tell Donna the good news.

In the car, I talked to myself once more. "I wonder how far I would have gone if the answer had been no? Sometimes I wish I'd never even told them about the wedding and just taken her myself. It's my free time. I'd hate to think it might have come down to my defying authority and going anyway! That's not my style. Thankfully I don't have to consider that after all."

Later I said, "We found you a volunteer, Donna. Guess who it's going to be," I told her.

Donna looked up quizzically, shaking her head.

"Me!"

"You? Oh, great!" The now familiar little giggle sealed the deal. She squeezed my hand and I felt her relief. How could she not feel more comfortable, knowing the one person who knew her illness best, was going to be on hand? After this, Donna began to relax and we concentrated on building up her strength and controlling her nausea.

The wedding was scheduled for five o'clock on a Friday with a reception immediately following. The bride and groom had arranged the reception a few blocks from where Donna lived. I knew it was dubious I could count on my day being calm enough I could make the wedding. "I'll be at the reception waiting for you when you arrive. I know I can get things set up mid afternoon, and rest assured, I'll be there before you are." We went over details and schedule with our aide and reviewed all the logistics.

"I'm not worried you'll come. But there's one thing, Joy. I'll be wearing a long blonde wig. You may not recognize me."

"Sure I will, Donna. You'll be the beautiful lady in the shiny new wheelchair."

Donna's two youngest sons picked her up and took her to the wedding at the university chapel, from where so recently the groom had graduated. The shiny new wheelchair fit neatly into the trunk, and it was safe for me to concentrate on setting up the cot for Donna at the reception.

As I had promised, I was waiting at the restaurant for the wedding party and family to arrive. Having checked and rechecked all the arrangements, I felt ready for whatever the evening brought.

Three very excited children, neatly scrubbed and shiny in their very best clothes, skipped up the stairs, followed by laughing parents doing their best to rein in the exuberance. Right behind them Donna arrived with her two youngest sons.

She stepped from the car, composed and smiling, her long blond hair curling around her joyous face, looking the very picture of good health. Together, the boys and I put her in the wheelchair and took her into the party house. Carefully the two boys lifted their precious charge in her wheelchair and easily took her up the stairs and to her temporary bed all made up and waiting just down the hall from the reception. Together we checked the reception room, sneaking a preview of the decorations before we settled her for a rest. We learned there was another party being held across the hall, a stag party.

The radiantly beautiful Donna, with joy and excitement shining through her face, made my heart skip with happiness.

"Joy, the wedding was lovely. Sorry you couldn't get there."

"Tell me all about it. You must need to lie down for a bit," I offered. Nodding, she stretched out on the cot to rest, covered lightly by the mohair cover we'd packed. Her family gathered around her, sharing in the evening's festivities and reveling in the presence, almost a miracle in itself, of their mother at the wedding. Their easy laughter and happy sounds filled the time as they talked about the wedding. Donna glowed with happiness and the laughter was constant, as they reminisced together.

I had not met most of her family. They all worked during the days and that meant they visited their mom in the
evening when I wasn't with her. Her three oldest grandchildren gathered around her, barely able to contain their
excitement at being at a wedding and with their grandma,
while Donna's two youngest sons squatted beside the cot to
be able to talk with her more directly. The beautiful picture
of family love made my heart smile.

Deeply touched by their joy, I slipped out of the room.
Memories of tonight would be precious for all the years to
come, and I wanted to give them a few moments of privacy to cherish, knowing the painful time that lie ahead.

When I returned, it was to tell Donna it was time for the
receiving line. Laughing family members said, "Wait until
you hear this." I wondered what was coming. "Mom's stock-
ing feet were sticking out here at the doorway. One of the
guests at the stag party came over and said, 'What's going on
over here?' It was too funny!"

Donna was laughing in sheer delight.

"Donna! I'm going to have to stand guard over your
body," I told her, between chuckles.

The room cleared while I helped her freshen her make-
up. "Look what I got," she said. With a mixture of pride and
shyness she handed me a small plaque with a red rose on it
and the words: To My Mother. You've always been there for
me, through all the times good and bad. I've never told you
how much you mean to me before. Let me tell you now.
Thanks, Mom, for giving me life and all you have. I'm so
glad you are my mother.

Tears of joy glistened in her eyes.

"Oh, Donna. That's beautiful! Who gave that to you?"

"My youngest son. He was only sixteen when I divorced

and I knew that had always been so hard on him. He said he wasn't good with words, so he was going to let this say it for him." I hugged her tightly as we hung onto this magical moment.

Donna broke into a joyous smile, sitting in her shiny new wheelchair in the receiving line. I introduced myself to the bride and groom and her parents.

"You take real good care of her," said the bride's mother.

"I'll do my best."

Guests gathered in the buffet line. We sat at a round table with one of her sons, his wife, and their three small children, aged three, five and eight. All scrubbed and shining in their best clothes they wiggled in excited anticipation. Donna moved out of her wheelchair, exhilarated to be joining her family for the celebration she almost missed. I bent to tuck my bag of emergency supplies under the table, but I was betting on not needing them. My fiancé had been invited to be a guest at the reception, too, and I watched Donna's face glow as he joined us.

Leaning over to her I whispered, "Your tummy medicine doing its job?"

Her eyes twinkled at me as she said, "So far." We exchanged thumbs up signs. She would try eating some of the food. Her daughter fixed her a plate of food with some of everything on it. She tasted it all.

Dancing followed and Donna sat there watching contentedly as all her family and I danced to the beautiful music played by a five-piece dance band. We had arranged private signals in case she needed anything, and after one number she quietly told me, "I think I'd better have a little rest." Placing her in the wheelchair, I rolled her back to the small cot waiting for her.

"Do you think you could sleep if I step out?" I asked, after settling her into the pillows and tucking in her mohair throw. She nodded and I closed the door, mindful of the stag party across the hall. Sitting near the door of the reception I checked her frequently while monitoring the evening for moments she would not want to miss.

The nap was short, but just the refreshment she needed, and Donna returned to the party. The photographer came and took pictures of Donna with all her family. I popped up and using her camera snapped photos of all the family members as they came over and visited with Donna, knowing how precious the last photos become. The wedding cake was served. A steady stream of family and friends found their way to her table to share time with her. The dancing went on and all the little children got into the act. A vibrant Donna laughed at their antics, a proud grandmother in full form. Knowing Donna wanted to feel like anything but a carefully tended patient resembling a hothouse plant, I happily popped up and danced now and then.

"You have a wonderful family and you did a great job with them. You must be so proud."

"Oh, I am! There were some hard moments when I wondered if I'd make it and I worried a lot, but they've all turned out so well. I'm proud of every last one of them."

Her emotions radiated in all directions as she sat at the reception. I monitored her for sudden fatigue but she had seemingly unlimited energy and it carried her through the evening.

The bride came over to Donna with a large bouquet of roses, gladiolas, and ivy from the wedding. "Mom, I'd like you to have these to take home." Donna beamed her gratitude and proudly held the bouquet on her lap.

"How are we going to get them home?" she asked the boys.

"We'll find a way," said her sons. Together we helped Donna into the car and loaded her wheelchair and flowers into the trunk. I blew her a kiss, as she closed the car door and drove away. I was teary-eyed as I watched them pull away. She was well enough that I knew they could manage tucking her in without me, and I didn't want to intrude on the moment that was certain to remain an important memory for all of them.

The next week our visits were full of wedding talk and the joy of the special night, while the beautiful bouquet of wedding flowers rested on the mantle, a daily reminder of the celebration Donna had been able to attend after all. They stood as testimony to the magic possible when one stays positive in the face of defeat. It was a week of contented sounds, easy conversation, and a feeling of all is well. We were grateful for the reprieve, as now Donna began to decline rapidly.

It started with weakness, which became a problem when she fell in the night. She had lain on the floor unable to get up until her morning aide came to care for her. Fortunately, she was not injured, but we knew we needed different arrangements for the time ahead.

"You have such a loving family. There are enough of them to share and help out. How about we ask them to each stay one night with you, taking turns, so you don't have to be alone any longer? That way no one will become too tired to work the next day. You'll be safe, but you won't need to feel guilty." I reached out and gently touched her, wanting to cushion the acknowledgement that her independence was nearly over.

Donna nodded. She had always looked after them. Now the tables were turned, and it was difficult.

I called her daughter. "Janeen, we need some help. Can you come over so we can talk about some ways to make your mom's nights safer?"

"Be right there," she replied. I knew Janeen would see that our schedule was carried out, and together we mobilized a plan that meant her mother would no longer be alone at night. On each visit Donna reported to me who stayed the night before, and for the moment, she felt infinitely more secure.

That bought time for us, and Donna had a chance to wrap up legal matters and detail how she wanted her affairs managed. Our agency supplied a social worker to visit and fill in all the missing gaps with up-to-date information Donna could not have known, and clearly didn't have the energy to research. I increased home health aide hours for the days and the family covered evening and night hours as soon as their jobs were done for the day. Donna began to talk about dying.

"I'm not afraid to die," she said in her even tone. "It's not that I want to. I was looking forward to a better time. But if that's not how it's going to be, then I have to accept that is the way it is." Her face was peaceful and I felt a burst of admiration as I saw that she had worked through her emotions and conflict to move into acceptance. Something had helped her achieve the ability to accept her fate with such solid adjustment.

"How is it you have acquired such wisdom, Donna? Sounds like you've lost some people and really thought about this."

"My parents, and last year my sister died from cancer." She looked at me with her enormous eyes, no trace of what she had experienced in her gaze.

"Tell me about losing your sister, Donna."

"It was really lonely for a long time, as she was always there for me to talk to and it was hard not to have that." She paused, her face no clue to her loneliness, but she took a deep breath and her chin quivered. "I still miss her, but I had to accept that is the way it is. I can feel her presence at times, right here with me." She lay quietly against the pillows on the couch, face impassive, as I wondered if there had even been time to finish grieving before her own loss began.

"I believe life goes on and all that," she went on. "I feel I'll see her again. Just a little sooner than I thought." She smiled sadly and looked down, allowing herself what I thought was a brief moment of regret.

"I'm sorry you lost your sister. That's tough. But how nice you can believe as you do, and know in your heart you'll be together again. I believe that, too." I reached out and held her hand, feeling a mixture of emotions.

"I guess you just do what you have to do," she stated. Her drooping eyelids told me she was tired so I brought our visit to a close.

It was almost two weeks from the wedding when one afternoon I arrived to find Donna in severe pain, speech slowed from her existing medications, and again in crisis. With a start I noticed her skin had a yellow cast to it and the whites of her eyes were streaked with yellow, too. She had fallen the night before, and had her son not been there to carry her to her bed, she would have lain on the floor all night once more, until daylight when enquiring loved ones rescued her. The amount of medicine now required to control her pain put Donna at risk for falling. Her safety was clearly an issue.

"Donna, we need to think about going into the inpatient hospice unit," I told her. "There we can have options for pain control we can't manage in the home, and you'll be safe. May I call your family and make the arrangements?" Her eyes met mine steadily for a moment, and slowly, in silence, she nodded her permission.

Her dream of staying home was gone, snuffed out without warning in spite of our best efforts. I was betting on her practical nature sizing up the situation and responding, as she had all her life, doing what had to be done. I phoned Donna's doctor and secured permission to transfer her to the unit.

Once more I turned to Janeen, working but a block away. I knew her well by then, and that was an ever-greater gift now that everything was changing so rapidly. "Janeen, I'm sorry to bother you. Would it be possible for you to leave work for a little bit and come talk with your mom and me?" I heard the sharp breath of concern.

Do I tell her on the phone or wait until she comes over? I thought. Better tell her. It's so hard to not know what an emergency call is about. She's level-headed and she'll be able to handle it.

"I don't want to upset you and give you a scare. It's just that your mom is having more pain, as you probably know. I think we could make her more comfortable in the hospice unit. You can all go with her, and still stay nights, or whatever, just like you do here, but we have more choices to help her with the pain there. I need to talk this through with you."

I heard a sigh of relief on the other end of the line.

"Give me five minutes and I'll be right there," she replied.

I'm so glad I told her! I thought. She must have been afraid I was calling to say it was all over.

Janeen arrived, and almost every one of her brothers arrived, too. "I gave them all a quick call," she admitted, with a sheepish grin. I was touched at how quickly she'd mobilized the family.

"Rick and Mandy just got back from their honeymoon today. They'll meet us there," she went on. I caught my breath, as I speculated what it must feel like to come home from your honeymoon to find such serious decline. We held our conference in the kitchen where Donna couldn't hear us, so that her rapidly eroding strength would be spared for the journey ahead. There were bound to be emotional reactions as her children faced the sudden realization their mother was much closer to death than they had realized. They needed a chance to adjust to the fear that knowledge would bring.

"We need to talk about what's happening right now," I began. "You have all been doing a really good job staying with your mom. But there have been some changes in her condition which I'm sure you've noticed." Silently they nodded. "Her condition is worsening and her time to die is drawing near. We haven't had time to talk about what you know about death. I know you've lost some family members before. We need to talk about dying." I shared with them my metaphor of car and driver to begin the important task of preparing them for the painful moments ahead.

"Your mom and I have talked a great deal about this. She is not afraid to die, and feels she will be with her sister and her parents." I paused to monitor their reactions. Silence greeted me, as this painful moment seemed to drop out of time and stand still. "I don't think that will happen today, but she is in terrible pain. We have options to help her in the inpatient unit that we don't have here. I would like to take her there and she is willing to go. The doctor also agrees it is best. You will all be able to be with her as much of the time as you wish. You can even go on staying with her nights. You've been doing such a wonderful job and I have been so pleased."

Janeen and her husband embraced, sharing the moment of sadness. One of the boys leaned against the refrigerator to steady himself, shock showing on his face at the realization of what was happening to his mother. The other sons looked to the floor, trying to hide the tears that were welling up in their eyes.

I went on talking about how much their being there for their mother had meant to her. I let them know how much comfort and protection Donna had felt, for I knew when the moments left are precariously few, no amount of effort feels adequate. They needed to hear from another that it had made so much difference.

"When it is time for your mother to die, I want you to know we will tell you everything we see happening to help you understand. Contrary to the public view, I have come to see that death is a highly underrated beautiful spiritual experience. Donna believes that, too, and we will do everything in our power to help it be so for her and you as well. With good pain control, there is every good reason to believe it will be peaceful and we will be able to make her comfortable."

Amid misty eyes and some cleared throats we talked about the dying process. We shared information regarding near death experiences and the important information these people report. They too knew people who had near death experiences and they shared their stories with me.

I looked around the group at the serious faces to see how they were doing. They met my gaze, their eyes dropping long enough to wipe a tear, and then one son asked, "Will she be coming home again?"

Thank God I got to know them all at the reception, I thought. Otherwise, this moment would be so much harder for all of us.

"I could be wrong, but I don't expect Donna will be able to come home again. She may be near liver shutdown and may possibly go into a coma. But we will do our very best to keep her comfortable. The staff on the unit is wonderful. They will surround your mother with love and take excellent care of her."

I outlined their options as a family who wished to be present and helping, inviting them to participate as completely as they felt called to do. "There's even a hot tub where she can have a whirlpool bath to soothe her if she wants." Only the kitchen clock could be heard as it ticked away the moments, while everyone struggled to understand how everything in life was about to change.

"Your mother is very proud of all of you. She has told me so many times and especially at the wedding. I am so glad you all had that wonderful time together. It has meant so much to you, I know. And it meant everything to Donna."

It was a bittersweet moment we wished we could have skipped. There were quiet tears. I reflected that I knew from whom they had learned to quietly accept what is. One said, "She's always been there for us. It's hard to know soon we won't be able to even see her again." The pain of those words went right to my heart.

"Your mother has told me she has been able to feel her sister's presence since she died. It's important to stay open to the possibility. Many people do, and they manage to feel the presence of their special loved ones after their deaths. You all are so close to your mother. Trust that even if you can't see her, she will be able to see you, as our near death survivors tell us happens." Once more the ticking clock filled the silence. Sad faces registered the unacceptable reality thrust without warning into this day.

"It's not that you or anyone could have done anything differently. It is that with all we know in medicine we have so much more to learn. We don't know how to fix bodies, when the cancer grows as rampantly as it is now growing in her body."

I felt tears slide down my cheeks. "Sometimes you cry, Joy. No need to hide the tears. It just shows you care," I told myself.

I answered questions, and then, decisively, they prepared to take her to the hospice unit, doing the one thing they knew could help now. It was decided Donna would ride in one of their cars. "I'd rather not go by ambulance if I have a choice," Donna had stated firmly when we asked.

"We can get you there, Mom," came a chorus of voices.

I made the phone arrangements and let the hospice unit know we were leaving soon. We gathered together a few belongings, including the plaque with a rose that said TO MOTHER. One of her sons picked her up and lovingly carried her to the car.

Our cars formed a caravan, with my car leading the way to the hospital. In the pain of the moment no one was absorbing directions. It's a condition I knew well. I wanted to see Donna settled into the unit and it was important I connect with the newly arrived bride and groom. I provided a familiar face in the suddenly unfamiliar, and they would need to catch up on the harsh changes that happened while they were away. Amid tears and sadness, we wound our way to the hospice building, driving slowly, to ease Donna's pain over the bumps.

Could it be only two weeks ago when we were so happy, I thought. How grateful I am we have that wonderful night to remember.

We eased Donna carefully into her bed on the hospice unit, introducing her to her final home. I greeted the tearful bride and groom who were waiting there for us, and caught them up on developments and most of the talk we had all shared in the kitchen at Donna's apartment. Knowing I could do no more, I left. It was out of my hands now.

Over the next few days, pictures of the wedding and of other family gatherings appeared in Donna's room. A video of the missed graduation was shown. Drawings from the grandchildren adorned the wall. Janeen and one of her sisters-in-law went through a whole box of photos to find pictures of how she usually looked and hung them up for all to see. Donna's pain was eased, as I had hoped, and the family continued to take turns staying with her, as best they could around their jobs.

With our encouragement the grandchildren were allowed to come and say good-bye to Grandma and spend time with their parents who wished to be close for their mother. The children's visits on such a warm and homey floor, looking much more like a hotel than a hospital, could help ease their grief, too, and take away the fear little children so often experience without our even realizing it. Best of all, for brief moments Donna was lifted back into the pride of being a grandmother, away from the awful truth that her life with them was almost over.

When I visited, I saw the progress they were making. There was pain, and growth, and tears and love everywhere. Connected as we were from our evening at the wedding, her children poured out their concerns to me and allowed themselves to be comforted by my observations and experience. Gamely they followed every suggestion I could make to help their mother and each other, but with pride I noted how they felt free to follow their instincts and institute their own touches naturally, in a way no one can teach others to do.

Donna, pain now deftly managed, died peacefully as I had felt she would, almost two weeks later, surrounded by her family in loving support, with pictures on the wall and a plaque with a rose at her bedside. The phone call came to let me know as I had requested.

Hanging up the phone, I remembered how beautiful Donna had looked, sitting in her shiny wheelchair, surrounded by her children and grandchildren, and the happy event I had been privileged enough to witness. I thought of the loving family unit she had created in spite of the hard times. I thought about all the time ahead that was not to be.

Sometimes you cry.

Support

I never ask the wounded person how he feels; I myself become the wounded person.

~ Walt Whitman

Snowflakes were falling yet again, in an unmistakably persistent winter already plagued by huge snowdrifts and icy inconvenience. Large flakes spoke eloquently of the season's beauty as they tumbled to earth from an overcast sky. I hopped out of my car and walked quickly to the small farmhouse, chuckling with childlike wonder at the flakes. Brushing my face with a damp mitten, I scurried for shelter as one flake landed on my nose. I laughed aloud and thought, What an appropriate metaphor for this family who really knows how to enjoy life.

I was about to enter a home filled with laughter and love that lifted my day. I always looked forward to my next visit and the caring I could count on finding. Knocking on the door I called out, "Hello, it's Joy!" and let myself in through the back door of the house.

As usual, several adult children were in the large kitchen, sharing freshly made donuts. Laughter and conversation filled the air. Not only did Ken have six children of his own, but he and his wife had helped raise his deceased brother and wife's six children. They had all bonded so successfully that they worked together not as cousins, but as one happy family. As I met each of them over time, I was laughingly assured over and over, "I am the favorite daughter (or son)" and heard this so often it automatically brought a chuckle. Obviously this was a familiar family running gag. That could only happen when people are really secure with their place in the family, I thought. What an accomplishment!

That particular snowy day I had an appointment to discuss Ken's situation with him and some of his family members. At the end of my last visit I had laughingly reminded Ken we had a date for ten a.m. the next day and his wife had asked him, "Would you like me to go out for the day so you can have a date?" Their easy repartee with each other was a joy to see and a clue to the easy manner with which they had approached raising so many children. Now both Ken and Emily were in their eighties, but the kitchen of the farm house was filled with youthful vitality, and still served up delicious homemade bread and donuts that Emily produced regularly. "I came to get my donuts, too, like you gave to Marcia," kidded one of the girls. I noticed the eyes dancing with mischief as they pretended to be jealous of one another. The gleeful laughter that erupted spoke volumes for the equality they truly felt. How wonderful to be able to pretend sibling rivalry and not feel it. Now there's a twist on life, I thought.

Our topic for discussion was the care Ken needed and how we could best meet his needs. He had come home from the hospital recently and was having radiation treatments for the rapidly spreading lung cancer he was experiencing, but the last two treatments had been canceled by the family when they realized their dad was not physically up to receiving them.

"We need to talk," said one son, "about how we decide what to do next. There will be a family conference tonight and we need to come to a consensus about which direction we are going." One of the strengths of this family was its ability to talk, and this was not the first time they had met to pool their efforts to problem solve for their father.

"It seems like Dad just isn't able to take these treatments," Ken Jr. said to me in the kitchen. "Most of us agree we don't want him to have to do anything that is going to rob him of his last little bit of time. Can you guide me as to what all we should be considering tonight?" I looked at his calm and thoughtful facial expression and admired the way he was considering the options. The well-worn list of suggestions held in his hand contained many scratched out items, and his pencil was held poised to add anything I suggested to the list.

We talked about the pros and cons of continuing treatment. Radiation was begun following just such a family-patient conference, during which they all decided they would feel much better if they gave the treatments a good try to see whether they would help or not. Carefully I reviewed with him what their doctor had said about the treatments, eliciting their expectations for possible effects from radiation, and how they could come to a responsible decision about their next step.

"I don't disagree with what you've done, canceling the last two treatments, based on what you have told me about how worn out your dad was from coming home from the hospital. We forget to warn patients just how fatiguing that really can be. Listening to the rhythm of his body and letting him have the additional rest was just right."

"That's good to hear. It's hard to know what to do at times but it seemed like the sensible thing to do."

"You know, common sense really dictates a great deal of what we do or don't do. Of course, it's really misnamed. It's uncommon sense anymore, but you all have it." We laughed good-naturedly, and I patted him on the upper arm. I meant what I had said, and I wanted him to feel comfortable with his own ability to make sensible decisions.

"So don't be afraid to listen to what your good sense tells you as you just did. On the other hand, you do really need to make this decision with your doctor since he's the one who fully can answer your questions. Good job that you've scheduled a conference with the whole family. The next step will be to let your doctor know what you decide."

"I have the feeling from our previous meetings the doctor will accept our input. Seems like he appreciates the whole family pulling together."

Walking into the living room I saw two other sons and a daughter were with their father, and Emily, in her grandmother's chair, was smiling proudly as she always did as she watched her husband surrounded by his family. "Well, Ken, did you remember our big date?" I queried.

"You bet. Spiffed all up for it with a haircut and everything." We laughed and shared our joke. What a wonderful way to live, I thought. Laugh first; react later.

Sitting in a chair by Ken's bed we began the group discussion. "Guess it's time to talk about what's next, Ken," I began.

"We are wondering about the radiation treatments." Ken Jr. led the discussion. "Dad's not been well enough to go the past two days and we need to make a decision about what next. In fact, we're not sure it's a good idea to continue them if it's going to take so much out of Dad to just get there and back."

"What do you think about all this, Ken?" I turned the question back to him. "Tell us how you think things are going."

"Not too good as far as I can see." I looked into his steady calm gaze and admired his open acceptance of life as it really was, not as he hoped it would be.

"Tell me what that means for you." I wanted to be certain he talked about his situation, for I knew from the past, Ken was not a complainer. If left to himself he would skip telling me just how badly he really felt.

"Well, I'm not getting any better. In fact, it seems like I'm worse every day. I know I'm going to die, and it just doesn't seem right to push to get to treatments that aren't going to do any good if it's going to make me so worn out. Seems like I ought to be spending my time and efforts enjoying the gang here instead." I thought, There is something about living on the farm, where weather and seasons must be honored, that prepared people for acceptance that what is just is.

"Your honesty is very helpful to all of us, Ken. Do I understand correctly that you would prefer to stop treatment and spend your time home with your loving family?" I restated his words to make certain we all had heard correctly.

Nodding, Ken went on. "I've had a good life. Almost eighty-eight years isn't bad. Everyone's going to die sooner or later. Guess this is just my time."

I felt a rush of compassion and took his hand. "One thing to remember, Ken. You are not going to die. Only your body dies. You will be just fine." I shared with him my analogy of the car and driver. "It's good there is a way to leave a vehicle that is no longer able to be repaired. Otherwise, it would be just like being in the desert in a car that was broken down and having no way to go anywhere."

He cocked his head slightly, his eyes wide and shining with discovery, and said, "I'll remember that."

"If I know you, Dad, if you think that new vehicle is going to be a shiny new Buick you'll be right there when they say the word." Ken, Jr. grinned impishly at his father.

Ken laughed and settled back into his pillows. "Sounds like a good choice to me!"

I knew I needed to teach them about the hospice service, which was open to them if the direction of tonight's family-patient conference finalized stopping radiation treatments. With Ken's clearly stated understanding of his waning condition and ready acceptance "everyone has to die sometime," it seemed the likely outcome from their search for new direction. I knew his breathing had deteriorated enough that we could expect some sudden changes that they needed to hear about, before unexpected emergencies caught them off guard. It was one thing to be able to adjust to life as it came, and a totally different one to be emotionally prepared for the inevitable changes just ahead. The only way to avoid some of the scary moments that could happen was to prepare them for this new direction in Ken's care before an emergency happened. They have come together to examine their options at just the right moment, I thought, before a sudden emergency forces the decision for them. How I admire their willingness to grapple with all this, together in sadness as they are in joy.

"One of the best advantages of hospice is that we do everything we can to help you stay comfortably right here in your home where you want to be. Should things develop so that isn't really feasible, which it does in a small percentage of cases, we have the back-up of our inpatient hospice unit, where there are nurses and medical personnel around the clock who can give you care."

"What kind of things might happen that we would want the unit?" Ken Jr. rubbed his forehead as he contemplated the possibilities.

"Actually, the most likely change for Ken would be that his breathing would become more difficult. There we have the added bonus of being able to administer medications that must be injected, and treatments administered by a respiratory therapist who handles such emergencies. That includes the highly trained personnel and equipment needed at our fingertips, and the quick access to methods to ease his breathing. We would be able to make him more comfortable in an efficient manner. Some treatments just can't be duplicated in the home."

Easily the family discussed this option, asking pertinent questions and interfacing with the discussion so that they would enter tonight's family conference well informed. I reassured them arrangements could be made for their mother to be present in the hospice unit with Ken, if that became necessary.

"They even have fold out beds she can sleep on so she would be right next to him, as she has always been." I watched in admiration as their body postures remained relaxed and they respectfully considered one another's input. What a treat to see how well it can happen when everyone pulls together and there are no hidden needs for someone to have all the control, I thought. This moment would make a great teaching tape.

"Any questions about anything else?"

"Just one thing. Last evening when he was having a coughing spell we turned up the oxygen setting. I'm assuming that's all right?" The statement was half question, half statement, and Ken, Jr. raised one eyebrow as he waited for my answer.

Nodding, I reassured them once again their good sense had been correct. "Do let us know if you must dial up to the top setting, and there is no higher to go. The home concentrators only go to five liters and if he needs all the oxygen that is available, we need to know so we can be prepared to help you further. It is one of the reasons we might take someone into the hospice inpatient unit, as there we have options for delivering a higher percentage of oxygen."

Carefully I taught them some elementary knowledge about breathing and what symptoms they might expect to see. "If he does start breathing very hard, or his color becomes dusky or blue, don't forget you can phone our on-call number anytime of the day or night." I pointed to the number I had posted by the phone as I spoke. "A nurse will help you right away and give you instructions what to do. It'll be a whole lot less scary to remember you have help night or day."

"I noticed he perspired a lot with this but his forehead was cold. Why is that?" one son asked.

"Well, the body can adjust to many needs but the most prevalent one is to be certain that blood is preserved for the heart, lungs, and brain. To do that it can cut down the circulation to the extremities, skin, and not so vital organs. You might say, the body made an executive decision that the skin could wait." Again we laughed, I enjoying the opportunity to be natural with this very open family.

"Now there's an explanation I can understand!" Family members shifted comfortably in their chairs as we returned to the familiar pattern of handling life's seriousness with a dash of humor. We continued talking about other concerns they were experiencing.

"Let me tell you, I admire how well this entire family is doing with all of this. You really are remarkable the way you pull together. I wish I could take a video of this to show people what can be accomplished."

"We've been through a few things during the years," said Ken Jr.

"I'll say! Tell her what happened when you were a kid," Emily prompted.

Pulling up his sleeve, Ken Jr. said, "Dad saved my life when I was fourteen. I was electrocuted when I stepped on a fallen power line I didn't see in a storm. My sister ran home to the barn and Dad came running and pulled me off the wire." He pointed to thick, long scars on his arm. "I was in the hospital for a long time and haven't any muscles where the electricity went into my arm. It came out here in my leg." Pulling up his pant leg he showed me the scar on his leg that marked the exit of all that electricity.

I shuddered. "Wow! That must have been some scene. What kept you safe, Ken? How did you pull him off the wire and not be electrocuted yourself?" I turned back to Ken, who was lying quietly against the pillows, head elevated to assist his breathing.

"I had on rubber boots and that must have saved me. At least that's what they speculated at the time."

How does anyone think that fast? What could it possibly have felt like to know your son was down on a live wire? I wondered.

Ken continued. "I figured I'd be electrocuted, too, so I reached over and pulled him up, jumping backwards at the same time so at least we'd both be back off the wire. I got him off, and, thanks to the boots I didn't get hurt. The good Lord was sure with me." It was almost too much to grasp that he had remained so calm and purposeful.

Ken Jr. spoke next. "Six years ago, my son, who was in the Navy was accidentally electrocuted while on duty."

My face must have registered shock. "What an irony. You were almost electrocuted, and then lost your son to electrocution?"

"In fact, the current I took was much more than what killed him. No one can explain why I lived and he didn't. It's been one of the things we've just had to accept."

I learned Ken Jr. and his wife had started a support group in their city in a Midwestern state for people who had lost a child. They continued to be active with recently bereaved parents. Less than two years ago her mother had died in a hospice program in yet another state. "It takes such a long time to get over losing someone, particularly a child," they agreed. We talked about the feelings that have to come out as part of the healing process, feelings of sadness, anger, regret, and sorrow.

Other family losses emerged also and that reminded me of the past, when the family had dealt with the untimely loss of Ken's brother and wife in an auto accident. Ken and Emily never hesitated to take over care of their children and create one homogenous family. The pattern for just pulling together and doing the best you could with what life dealt you was set back then, I thought. I shook my head in wonder.

"You didn't by any chance have a near-death experience when you were electrocuted, did you?" It was a hunch that began to tug at my mind, and now I turned in my chair so I could better study Ken Jr's face.

"As a matter of fact I did." He smiled at my excited reaction.

"Tell me about that."

"I saw myself floating above my body and everyone scurrying around to help me, then I went down a tunnel like you hear about. I passed into another one with incredible light and there were shadows around me of beings, angels or whatever. I couldn't see their faces but I felt their love and it was incredibly peaceful, just beautiful beyond words." He smiled as he remembered and his hands gestured as he spoke of the beauty.

"No wonder near-death survivors are so often a bit resentful when we succeed in bringing them back. It's so beautiful where they have gone." I had heard this so often that I felt I really did understand the ambivalence, on one hand knowing their work wasn't done, on the other, wanting the peace they had experienced to continue.

"Oh, yes. I can relate to that." Ken Jr. nodded his understanding. "At the time I was young and didn't know what I do now. But the experience always stayed with me and I recognize it was a powerful influence in ways I can't put into words."

Another son spoke up. "I also have had a similar experience. I didn't know I was sick but I woke up in the middle of the night and couldn't talk, saw a tunnel with a light at the end of it and found myself going down it. Many presences were there with me, and although I didn't see any of the faces clearly either, I was able to feel their help and knew I was not alone. It wasn't the least bit frightening. I just felt wonderful peace and love. The next thing I knew I had come back but the memory is still vivid for me."

This family is full of surprises, I thought. "How long ago was that?" I asked.

"A few years, maybe. I'm not certain what that was preparing me for but it stands out in my mind. And I know what you're saying to be true. It fits so well with my own experience."

Reluctantly, I gathered up my clipboard and nursing bag and prepared to go to my next visit. There was something so inviting about being in the presence of all this love and magnificent experience that I was in no hurry to leave. As I started out the kitchen door one of the sons-in-law followed me to talk further.

"You know, there's a story I want to tell you. A couple of years ago my sister lost her daughter at age thirty-four to cancer. She had an awful time accepting that her child was going to die, and when she finally did see that was going to happen, she really panicked. We kept vigil with her up in the hospital for a whole night and into the next day, sitting in a circle of chairs in the waiting room just outside her daughter's room in the intensive care unit.

"Suddenly a woman we didn't know came up and sat down beside my sister. 'The waiting is the hardest, isn't it?' she said. To tell you the truth, I kind of resented her intrusion on our tight little circle but my sister began talking with her. We hadn't been able to reach my sister to comfort her, so I was pleased someone else could get her to talk. 'I lost my son a few years ago, too,' she went on. 'I went into the chapel and prayed to God saying I knew how much he had suffered for us, losing his Son to help us. 'No you don't' came back the reply.' That made me think I wasn't alone.' My sister hung on to every word she said.

"The woman went on. 'By the time my son died, I saw the beautiful peace on his face and I knew he was to be all right and was with our God who understands everything.' They talked more, and to our surprise, my sister told the lady all her concerns and became calm for the first time. Eventually, the lady got up and walked down the hall away from us. I watched her go, and she just disappeared in front of my eyes." He paused, looking at me to gauge my reaction.

"You mean...?"

"She just disappeared while I watched her go. My chair had a perfect view of her going down the hall. I'm convinced she had to have been an angel. One of those encounters you read about but never expect to experience. Because after that, when my niece died a couple of hours later, my sister said, 'Did you see the beautiful little smile on her face? You could just tell she was at peace.' And from then on, she was fine. Still sad, but no longer locked into a painfully silent prison of grief." He smiled a tender smile, and shook his head as he remembered.

"There are really wonderful stories out there if we just collect them, aren't there? Thank you for sharing that with me."

"That's why I know what you're saying makes sense. There's too much evidence that something wonderful happens. I've seen it with my own eyes. A miracle."

Yes, miracles galore if we only suspend our disbelief long enough to see them, I thought. I knew that it said something important about him that he allowed himself to add it up for himself.

"I see these things as miracles, too. My feeling is that even though we can't prove them yet, it doesn't mean they aren't there. There was a day when scientists thought the earth was flat. Well, it was round and that didn't change just because we believed otherwise. Why not look at miracles that way, too? Your family certainly has had plenty of food for thought."

Swinging my little red car out the driveway I reflected on the conversations I had just had. The size of this family not only increased the possibilities for emergencies, it had increased the potential for extraordinary events, too. Thoughts of our time together and the events shared stayed with me as I wound my way back into the city, through crowded streets and busy intersections to visit my next patient.

I reached for the dial of my car radio and tuned into the middle of a talk show. The host was interviewing a French priest, who had lived forty years in the farthest north land of Canada as a missionary to the aboriginals there. "When I first arrived I thought I knew everything and had a lot to teach and little to learn," the Father stated. "We were two different cultures teaching each other. Each had a lot to give and to receive."

"How have you dealt with that, when the native belief has seemed to you to be at least as valid as your own?" asked the interviewer.

"When we talk in terms of spiritual growth all people meet at the level of spirituality which is beyond differences. I think religions are always based on divisions; divisions based on culture, on language, or on history. But spirituality is just like a big underground river and anybody can dig a well into that river. And at a spiritual level all people meet. That's what I have learned in the past forty years in the North."

Anyone can dig a well into the river of spirituality. What a profound belief, I thought. I arrived at my destination and reluctantly turned off the radio, wishing I could take time to ponder this exciting new thought. I didn't even know the name of the speaker who gave me this magnificent metaphor.

Parking on the street, carefully observing the alternate parking signs to avoid a fine, I swung the strap from my bag over my shoulder, locked my car and headed up the stairs to the front porch of an old rambling house. Once spacious and elegant it had seen happier days. It was now divided into rooms, and served as a boarding house. I had learned from past visits that it lacked functioning doorbells. "Just knock on the front left window as you walk by, and I'll let you in," Buddy had told me. The outside door provided access to a locked inner door that he opened for me. It was a system that clearly had limitations.

Buddy was largely bed ridden and tended to faithfully by a neighbor and fellow tenant who, although totally untrained in how to provide care to someone so ill, watched over his friend carefully. For twenty-eight years Buddy had lived in this room, with a communal bath across the hall and down three stairs. Fiercely independent, he'd outlived his wife by many years and had watched two younger sisters die from cancer. He managed to take care of himself with the assistance of his son who checked on him every few days, his assistance fulfilling tasks Buddy couldn't manage. This allowed him to continue to feel independent. In the few weeks I'd known this man, I'd learned he was the one in the boarding house who'd always had a car and over the years he took other boarders to work, to the grocery store, or on the errands not reachable by bus. When one of the tenants had lost his license, Buddy took him to work every day and picked him up so he wouldn't lose his job. Now he was unable to drive, and one of the others drove his car to get groceries for him. I admired how the guys really looked after each other with fierce loyalty.

Two days earlier I'd sent Buddy to the hospital to have fluid drained from his rapidly swelling abdomen. They had wanted to admit him to the hospital for additional treatment, but he adamantly refused to stay. "I'm going home to die in my own house," he had insisted. His son, Joe, who knew a lifetime of his father's insistence to do it his way, had supported his right to do so as long as he could manage. He brought Buddy back to his home of almost three decades.

"It isn't much, but it's my home," he'd told me defensively on our first visit. I sat in the only chair and reassured him I was fine and was not here to visit his house but to see how he was doing.

On this call, his neighbor, Edgar, was visiting and let me in. I suspected as much because Edgar's Belgian Shepherd and tiger cat were sitting on the porch. They usually signaled his presence. This dog and cat combo, with their non-adversarial relationship, mirrored the incongruity of the human friendships in the boardinghouse. Since Buddy's only son had to work, Edgar was a lifeline who prevented him from being unsafe, as he was no longer able get out of bed unassisted. Even with help it was an effort of diminishing returns. As long as I could establish he was in a safe situation, the law guaranteed a patient his choice to stay at home. Edgar was the lynchpin that made this plan work.

Not that I had much say in the matter. Buddy was clearly in charge. Unless I was forced to pull rank and insist to insure his safety, moving him anywhere was dependent on the decision he would allow a change in his care. I put that tactic on a back burner as a last resort. Stripping Buddy of his last bit of independence was the farthest thing from my desire.

I let my gaze sweep the one-room apartment and noted the small portable oven with door open to increase the heat in the apartment. What a contrast I'm seeing today, I thought. One case with the family and resources all smoothly working together, the next with very little family and the needs barely met. My eyes swung to the phone, now carefully placed by the bed where Buddy could reach it to summon Edgar for help.

"I checked him at two a.m. and then he called me at five-thirty and I got dressed and came over to help him again. I keep coming in. I've got keys and all that," Edgar reported. "He can't get up alone anymore. I keep some water by the bed for him to drink, and I take him to the bathroom."

"You're really making it possible for your friend to have his choice and still be here, Edgar. You're a wonderful friend and Buddy is lucky to have your help." I marveled to myself, Human kindness has the capacity to change everything for the one who receives it. That's even more important here where there are so few choices.

Buddy solemnly nodded his head, as he lay on his side, eyes closed, his wavy white hair spilling over the pillow. I felt a swell of emotion for these two men, separated in age by decades and light years apart in interests, but placed by fate in the same rooming house. Their relationship was based on mutual respect and mutual need.

"He's always done a lot to help me, too," came Edgar's quick reply. "We look out for one another. Once, a few years ago I lost my license for a while, and every day Buddy got up and took me to work so I wouldn't lose my job. Every time he went fishing he remembered me and brought me some." I was struck by Edgar's ability to call a spade a spade.

I said to myself, "We may live in a world that increasingly likes to posture, but today I'm seeing people who are willing to openly and honestly help one another. How refreshing it is to see genuine caring in action."

Finishing his report Edgar summed it all up. "Well, I'll go now for a while and let you examine him. I'll be out back in my place so just call if you need anything." Sliding the door closed behind him, he left Buddy's apartment, grasping the importance of his friend's privacy as easily as he grasped the need to maintain his independence.

I walked over to the bed and began examining my charge. His blood pressure was significantly lower, his heart rate much weaker, his breathing was more labored, and now he kept his eyes closed most of the time to save energy. Weakness had overtaken Buddy. I knew his ability to remain at home was evaporating rapidly, in spite of all his determination and courage, right before my eyes. Buddy began to talk of leaving his home of twenty-eight years.

"I need twenty-four hour care now," he said with authority.

I did a double take at this change in direction. "You refused to stay in the hospital when they wanted you to. Does that mean you've changed your mind and want to go back to the hospital?"

Buddy emphatically shook his head on the pillow, eyes still closed, his adamant expression unmistakable. "No!" he said. I sat down on the only chair in the apartment, mystified at how to proceed.

"Hospice," he stated. "You said someday I could go to hospice." I nodded, realizing this was Buddy's way of admitting he couldn't go on with his situation any longer. More than once he had refused to even consider this option. I was surprised at how pragmatic he became in the face of his newly realized limitations. Maybe that's how you've survived, Buddy, I thought, by knowing when to back down.

"Are you certain you're ready to go to the inpatient unit, Buddy? I can admit you to the hospice service; your son has said he will sign as your primary care giver, but only if you are absolutely certain that is what you wish to happen." Carefully I watched his face for indications he would change his mind again.

"I'm not going to get any better. Might as well go. I'm dying." Buddy allowed himself one small peek at my face to gauge my expression, then closed his eyes again. It was as if all sensory stimulation was too much for him now.

He may not have much longer, I thought. If he's ready to go in maybe he knows something instinctively he doesn't even recognize he knows. It certainly will help him die with the dignity that is so important to him, and I need to honor his wish now.

"I'll have to make arrangements for this, but if you're certain you've made up your mind I will do that. Your son won't be able to meet me here until after work but he's already said he will back whatever decision you make. I can easily come back, and we will call the ambulance and see you on your way to hospice." Just as adamantly as he had refused before, Buddy now agreed. I walked away from the bed to collect my nursing bag, then stopped and on a hunch went back to the bed.

"Buddy, are you seeing the white light?"

A suddenly much more alert Buddy shook his head no. "I don't think so," he replied.

"Or anyone you knew who has already passed away?"

Buddy shook his head and I thought about my next move. Something had made him change his direction. Kneeling by the bed I lightly touched his hand and looked directly into his face.

"Oh, I think a lot about my sisters who died from cancer and my wife. It's just like they are here talking to me but I don't think I see them."

"Well, you may see them eventually. Most people tell me they do when it gets nearer the time to die. It doesn't mean death will be any moment when you do. But, Buddy, they can be a good source of information for you. Those who die and we are able to resuscitate, who then remember what happened, tell us it is a wonderful journey filled with peace. Others are there to help as well. I just had two people in the same house tell me that not more than an hour ago."

My thoughts were racing. You're so independent, if I tell you to ask for help you're likely to go in the opposite direction. I need some inspiration here, to help you, Buddy, before this window of opportunity closes.

"When you do see them it is your right to receive instructions how to proceed. Just tell them 'I'm willing to do what I need to. Show me what to do.' They can teach you what to do and it's all right to be assisted. All the people I've been with when they die, who could still talk, told me they were being given instructions, so there will be help there for you, too."

Buddy opened his eyes and picked his head up off the pillow. The suddenly brightened, excited look on his face told me he heard every word I spoke. Nodding decisively he said, "I will. Thanks, dear." Visibly relieved, he laid his head back into the pillow.

"I'll make some calls to make the necessary arrangements, and then we should be able to admit you to the inpatient unit tonight."

"Tonight?" He picked up his head once more. "Oh, good!" With a small smile of satisfaction, he returned to his pose with eyes closed and relaxed into the pillow, now reassured his lonely vigil was about to end.

Calling Edgar, I relayed the change in plans and let him know I would be back at five o'clock. I made some additional preliminary calls, one to Buddy's son to set up our appointment time, others to his doctor and to the inpatient unit to save a bed. Once more I walked to the bed and checked Buddy's breathing and pulse. "I'll be back before long," I said softly, as I patted him lightly on the arm. "I'll meet your son here after work and we'll transfer you to hospice then."

To myself I reflected, "I wonder why these things always happen on a Friday? No way I'm not going to do this even though it means working late. Buddy may not have until Monday."

Buddy's son and I arrived simultaneously. "Good timing," I said as I offered my hand to him. Shaking hands we sized up each other, to see if the person we had talked to so many times on the phone looked like we each had imagined. I needed to prepare him for the dramatic changes in his father. I was grateful I had talked on the phone with him just twenty-four hours earlier, and learned how concerned he felt.

"Let me update you before we go into the house. Your father has gone down hill quite rapidly. You'll see some change from when you brought him home from the hospital two nights ago."

"He's pretty determined to do it himself." Buddy's son shook his head in patient resignation.

"Little did I dream your father would make the shift to another plan so readily." In my heart I knew this to be an emotional moment and empathy for what the son was facing flooded in me.

"Sounds like he's much weaker today. Edgar calls me frequently and keeps me filled in on his progress. When I talked to Dad on the phone I noticed he sounds quite changed." I could see he was prepared for the differences at least with a surface understanding, but seeing the decline would likely be a shock.

"I was surprised your father wished to have hospice service but I know that means we need to move right away. This can be a signal there might not be much time left. Are you prepared for that? I know this is being rather suddenly thrust upon you." I placed my hand lightly on his elbow in a gesture of the caring I felt.

"Actually I'm relieved he'll be going where he can have more care. When I brought him home from the hospital the other night I felt things were not as good by far as they used to be, so, in some ways I'm not surprised to hear what you are saying. I feel inadequate to take good care of him. There's not much more I can do here. I know he could have much better care somewhere else."

I couldn't help noticing the note of dejection that crept into his voice. "You've been doing a really good job of being there and helping in ways that didn't violate your dad's need for independence."

"Oh, that's good to hear! You wonder when you're doing it what you really should be doing. All my life he's been in charge. He's so headstrong it's not like I have much say about anything. I just try to take it one step at a time."

I noticed his jaw muscles tighten and pulse, and I wondered what battles of the past that tightness signaled. "That's usually the way we all have to proceed. Have you lost others? Tell me a little about your family." Gently I encouraged him, knowing I needed to know more about his loss history to help him with the imminent loss of his dad.

Conscious we were talking in the driveway he quickly told me about losing his mother more than twenty years earlier, his half sister from cancer many years ago, and his father's sisters, his aunts. "That's quite a few people to lose. I see you are no stranger to all of this. How are you doing with all you are having to handle?" His face looked calm, or, I wondered, was he just numb? He had the right to be with all that loss.

"Quite well, I guess. I kind of feel that if he has to suffer like he now seems to be, it will be easier to accept that he must pass on. Although it seems like it's going awfully fast all of a sudden." His simple statement perfectly summarized his conflicted feelings.

"Are you content then to sign as a primary care giver for your father? That is the key to his plan." I couldn't help note that Joe looked like he was accepting this news. Yet, on the other hand, I thought he was responding from a state of denial, saying the right words but not feeling the impact of what he knew. I wondered which emotion was going to win.

"If that's what my dad wants, I'm ready to do it." We moved out of the driveway and into the house. The ever-faithful Edgar was already there, waiting on his friend and staying available to let us in through the double doors that separated their world from the world of change they were about to experience. We worked our way through the necessary paperwork after establishing once more that Buddy was secure with his decision.

"You can still visit him in the hospice unit, Edgar, and so can the other friends that live here." I gave him directions to the hospice and carefully he wrote down street addresses, mileage, and the easiest route on a scrap of paper.

Following his instincts, Edgar moved to the bed and said, "Thanks for all the fish, Buddy. I'll take care of things here for you and try to get up to see you where you're going."

Buddy roused himself from closed eyes and half lifted off the pillow to touch hands with his friend. "Thanks for all that you've done for me, Edgar." Turning to his son he said, "Get a few dollars out of my pocket. Give him at least a ten." Joe hurried to comply with his father's wish, letting him make his own choices now as he always had done in the past.

"I don't need money, Buddy. I was glad to do it for you." Joe and I exchanged glances and stood back to let this poignant moment unfold naturally.

The ten-dollar bill was handed over to Edgar. "And give him whatever change is in my pocket. He did my laundry for me, even put his own sheets on my bed. I won't be needing them any longer."

For a moment Edgar looked like he might refuse the change, teetering on the edge of indecision. Then, understanding Buddy's need to be in the driver's seat and give one more time before all his strength evaporated, Edgar took the money and said simply, "Thanks, Buddy. That'll help a lot."

Shuffling his feet slightly, Edgar said, "One thing. Now that you're going into the hospice house I'm going to go for some treatment I need on Monday. Would it be all right if I use your car just one more time to get some groceries?"

Buddy digested the request, his reactions slowed now by weakness, and then nodding decisively said to his son, "Get him the keys. They are in my pocket." Turning to Edgar he said, "Just give them back to Joe when you return."

"Thank you, Edgar," I added, "for making it possible to give Buddy his wish and stay here as long as he could. You've been an immense help to me, too." I shook his hand, then gave him a hug.

"I was glad to help. I would have delayed my own going in for treatment a little if he needed it. He's always been here for me." We bid him good-bye and I wondered if Edgar was leaving to avoid having to see his friend exit the home in which he had been so determined to die. Edgar knew more than anyone else what heroic efforts it had taken to get this far. What is so much to receive is often very little to give in comparison, I thought. Somehow you knew that, Edgar.

Father and son worked out the remaining details that let him leave his home for the last time. "I'll come back and clean up for you tomorrow, Dad. Anything else you want to take with you now?"

Buddy shook his head, eyes again closed, resting on the pillow, his facial expression relaxed and accepting. Fate had dealt him no pension plan in spite of more than thirty-five years with the same company, the result of a fluke decision by management that was out of his control. Since then, being in charge of every nuance of his life had been incredibly important to him as the only way he could see to avoid trust being broken one more time. Now he was able to let it all go with the realization he would not need to stay in charge much longer.

Calling the ambulance company, I requested no lights or sirens. "This man would like to go to the hospice unit with dignity and simplicity," I related.

"Oh, we wouldn't do that to you. We'll be glad to make it a quiet ride. You're right around the corner from where we are now so and we'll be there in twenty minutes or less," they said.

Then I called the hospice unit. "He'll be arriving in a half hour or so. Buddy loves classical music and listens to it on the radio for hours. You might want to turn on the radio for him as soon as he's settled. His son will be up right behind him as soon as he parks the car."

I tried to turn on the porch light and the lights in the hallway only to discover there were no bulbs in either that worked. Stepping out on the porch I waved to the ambulance driver and readied my sheet of information to give them. The male and female two-person crew talked kindly to Buddy, who was still relaxed and willing to accept our instructions about his needs.

Patiently and carefully we helped Buddy stand and pivot, then lifted him to the stretcher. We wrapped his fragile frame in blankets and towels to keep out the cold. We rolled the stretcher out onto the porch, then lifted it down to the driveway and into the waiting ambulance.

Turning to Buddy's son I saw he was calm and composed. "You've done a great job of being there while allowing your father his choices, Joe," I said. In my heart I knew it was all going so fast he needed to hear this more than once.

"I hope so. I just do what I can and wonder how it really is. I don't know about these things." He sounded grateful for the reassurances and I remembered well the feeling of doing the best you could and wondering how well that was working.

"Take my word for it. You've been doing great with all the things that were needed but especially at accepting your father's need to have choices, his own choices. I'm not sure how you came to realize this when it seems so hard for most of us to understand, but never forget, for a moment, you gave your father that priceless gift." We shook hands and then spontaneously I hugged him. "Don't forget to look after yourself, Joe, and take care of your own needs."

We smiled, and he said, "Thanks, Joy. I'll give you a call and let you know how I'm doing in the future. I know you care and I've really appreciated all you've done to help my dad and me."

"My pleasure to help in any way I can. Good luck to you and your dad. They'll help him up in the unit as best they can and we should be able to make him comfortable, help him handle the pain. Let them assist you, too. We believe in being there for the whole family unit." Quickly I gathered my papers and nursing bag together, remembering to turn off the small oven whose heat was no longer needed to keep Buddy warm.

I moved to my car and turned to see Joe carefully locking his father's house. I stayed until he was in his car, then rolled down the window, and asked, "You know where he's going?" He nodded and we said one last good-bye for now. I hoped he would call and let me know how he was doing. I sensed that was important for both of us.

Alone once more in my car I reflected on the day which had provided such contrast and was now over at seven o'clock. We all needed each other no matter how independent we have been. That need doesn't stop when we leave this part of the world. I had seen firsthand the results of near death experiences and their impact. Am I ever glad we are starting to see information about how near death experiences help those who are about to die, I thought.

Monday morning at work my voice mail carried the message that Buddy had passed away in the early evening Saturday. So fast, I thought. I am so thankful I worked overtime and followed my hunches on that one.

Shortly later my phone rang. "Hi, Joy," came the voice that was clearly Buddy's son.

"I'm so pleased to hear from you, Joe. I am sorry to hear Buddy died on Saturday and a little surprised how soon that happened. How are you doing?"

"It was all so quick. I really didn't think it would be this fast."

"Tell me what happened." I encouraged him.

"Joy, it was beautiful just like you said it could be. He seemed relieved to not have to be in charge. I was taking my time doing chores that needed to be done on Saturday because I had no idea just what was happening. Do you know what he did, Joy?"

"What?"

"When I got up to his room I could hardly believe how much he'd changed in less than twenty-four hours! He could barely talk anymore but we managed to say good-bye to each other before he lost his voice completely. I was able to tell him how much he meant to me. His eyes were closed and he looked peaceful, with a small smile on his face. Then suddenly he put his hand up in the air and waved good-bye to me. Just like that he was gone."

"Thanks so much for seeing to it that I knew," I said, as I felt the catch of emotion in my throat. It was a caring gift Joe had given to me and I was touched.

"Thanks for everything, Joy. I know you worked late and everything to help my dad. I want you to know that meant a lot. To both of us."

"You're very welcome. Buddy didn't ask much of anyone. This was one time he did and he was more than due to get his wish."

Hanging up the phone I sat for a quiet moment, envisioning a smiling Buddy wave good-bye. Aloud I said, "Good for you that you did it your way. Happy journey, Buddy! From what I hear it's going to be wonderful."

Acceptance

*It all depends on how we look at things, and not on how they
are in themselves.*

~ Carl G. Jung

Perhaps it was the rakish purple hat on the teddy bear, or
the long dangle earrings swinging jauntily from each ear. I
had never seen a teddy bear with earrings before. Or possibly it was because Sir William the St. Bernard had the
nickname Will. I had never known a dog with a nickname
before either. In retrospect I could never decide what caught
my awareness and signaled this was to be a special experience. It could have been any one of a number of creative
aspects of this amazing household. Not that the unusual is
rare in my business. But right from the start I sensed this was
to be an important event for me.

Meeting Margaret was memorable in itself, as she was
obviously fueled by a zest for living that eighty years had
failed to dim. Her expressive face had surprisingly few wrinkles, and the broad, contagious grin that took over when she
smiled accentuated freckles that distinctively announced her
Irish heritage. It didn't matter that when I first saw her she

was lying in bed. That grin announced her zeal for life as surely as if she handed me an engraved announcement.

I introduced myself, and swung my nursing bag to the wooden chair at the foot of her bed. "Your daughter and I just met, and she is welcome to stay with us during the interview if you like." I smiled at Kate, a pretty woman in her early fifties, in whose home Margaret was now living. My paperwork indicated she had advanced cancer and had moved here from Florida to be with her daughter, since she was rapidly losing strength and now needed ongoing care.

"By the time I finish all these papers you're going to think I've moved in," I joked. "I'll do them as efficiently as I can manage, and hopefully not tire you too much." Rifling through my folder of papers I began my interview. Will had other ideas.

I have become used to the animals in the household checking me out when I arrive to care for my patients, knowing it's almost like a job interview and they want to make sure I'm on the up and up. I reached down and petted the St. Bernard's head as he looked into my eyes, and then laid his head in my lap.

"Will likes you," said Kate. "Is he annoying you? He doesn't usually warm up this quickly to strangers."

Shaking my head, I spoke directly to the dog. "Hey, Will. I'm on the team. You and I are going to work together to help Margaret." Will settled down at my feet, head resting on massive brown paws. And they say pets don't understand, I thought.

Steadily we edged our way through the myriad of details necessary to begin home care for a terminally ill person. In spite of the sparkle in her eyes, Margaret had the fragile look of someone whose energy is limited, and I monitored her closely to be certain she was not becoming worn out. Somewhere between the lists of past surgeries and current symptoms I asked casually, "What are your hobbies?"

Margaret laughed, her lively smile taking over her face. "Where do you want me to start?"

"Don't forget to tell her about the Dancing Grannies," reminded Kate. My interest now piqued, I looked up from my paperwork to see Margaret's eyes dancing with delight.

"You were a Dancing Granny?" I asked. My mind flashed to an image I had from television, when I had seen aerobic exercise routines performed to music by women in Florida, all of them in their golden years. "Isn't that a group from Florida?"

Nodding, Margaret shifted in the bed. "When I lived in Florida, before I became so ill, I was a member of the Dancing Grannies and we went all over sharing our routines with people. We were on television and performed at so many exciting places. It was great fun."

"Good for you! Sounds like show biz took a bite out of you in retirement."

Margaret tipped her head back a notch and laughed gleefully at the memories.

Smiling, I bent my head back to the paperwork and wrote down "member of Dancing Grannies." I thought that ought to bring some comments when my papers are reviewed.

"Tell me what work you have done and a little about yourself," I prompted. Mother and daughter exchanged glances and I noted they had the comfortable ambiance of truly good friends.

Slowly her story emerged. Born in the Bronx, Margaret was the mother of four daughters, living in the New York

City area, when her husband died suddenly from a heart attack. Two of her children were still young enough to be in school. She went back to school and obtained her Master's degree, becoming a teacher, to help keep her family together and provide for them more effectively.

"You must have been a wonderful teacher," I said, as a picture of a classroom filled with buoyant enthusiasm flashed before my eyes.

"She was," Kate said with pride. "She taught elementary school and the children loved her."

"Tell me more about yourself, your family, where you have lived, all those kinds of things."

"I am the oldest of six girls but only three of us are still alive. My youngest daughter died suddenly at age thirty-five from the complications of diabetes. Then after Kate's son drowned at age eleven, I moved here for about five years until finally, I retired and went to Florida."

My breath caught and I let out an explosive sigh. "Wow! You've been through a few things that tested the waters, haven't you?" Multiple losses I thought, and now she's here to be cared for by her daughter who has lost so many. I mentally said to the dog, "Will, we have our work cut out for us."

Margaret's smiling acknowledgment showed me she had made peace with the past. "I thought it was important for me to be here with Kate," she stated. "I couldn't imagine being anywhere else." Mother and daughter exchanged tender smiles that clearly announced the wonderful bond they had forged.

We moved through the rest of the visit smoothly, finishing just as Margaret began to wilt. "We'll save more conversation for other visits," I said. "I'm looking forward to being your nurse."

Our eyes met, her direct gaze assuring me we had accomplished a great deal for the first visit.

Over the next few weeks, Margaret and I developed an easy rapport as we talked about her favorite classroom stories and interesting places she had traveled. We laughed and joked in between the necessary symptom checks, handling pain control issues, and checking her blood pressure.

I never knew what I would find. Each week the resourceful Kate created new ways to brighten her mother's life in the home that was to be her last. Beautiful nature photos hung on the bedroom walls, brightening the view from the bed. Together they poured over old photo albums. Kate probed her mother's memories for special stories from the past and wrote them down, often to share the best ones during my visits. Wonderful poems appeared, as if by magic. "Kate has a knack for surrounding her mother with the significant past and beauty too," I reflected. "We could all take a lesson from her on that. She even does it with humor!"

Mother and daughter had formed an unmistakably tight understanding of each other. Margaret would think about closing the window. Kate would wordlessly rise and close it.

Kate was a daughter who possessed finely tuned instincts, uniquely expressed. She was the one who gave her mother the teddy bear, dressed it in fancy clothes and then added the outrageous purple earrings. Just looking at that teddy bear made us laugh. She wrote down sayings from her mother's childhood days in the Bronx. Things like "Gee golly gosh damn double hell spit Columbia."

"Did you really say that?" I asked.

Margaret laughed her trademark hearty laugh of sheer joy. "Yes, and we used to jump rope to "Holy Mary Mother of God. Chase the chickens out of the yard.""

Being witness to their capacity to reminisce so happily was a wonderful addition to my days, and I stepped away from the visit refreshed and invigorated.

They sang campfire songs and told favorite childhood stories. They unearthed the treasures of the past with a simple, "Do you remember when...?" That was all it took to launch them into another moment of merriment. They went beyond being on the same wavelength. They were kindred spirits bonded further by the unspeakable tragedies they had faced together.

Each visit surprised me in some way that lifted my own spirits as well. Always, Will was by the bed, guarding Margaret and checking me out.

One day I arrived to find my wonderful patient sound asleep, an occurrence that was happening more often. I sensed Kate's unease at the "quiet, do nothing times", as she called them.

"It's hard to have the quiet stretches, isn't it?"

"Oh, yes! The busy moments are easy; we have so much to share." Kate's drawn and worried expression and shaking hands told me just how uncomfortable it was.

"Tell me how are you dealing with the quiet times." I requested as gently as I could.

"Well, not too well some days, to be honest. I'm just doing some projects to fill the time, so I'll be here when she wakes up." She paused, obviously uneasy. "And thinking." Her voice trailed off and her gaze was far away.

"About?"

"The time ahead, hoping I'll be equal to it. I know all too well it can be pretty rough." One lone tear started down her flushed cheek.

I let the moment have its due. "Each loss has its own special challenge, Kate. Yet, we learn from, and can draw upon the wisdom we've gained from other losses." I paused, searching for just the right words. "While you keep your fingers busy, allow yourself to remember the strong moments you've had, too. You aren't going to change who you are in life. You have shown yourself how strong you can be even when the going is terribly tough. It is part of the fabric that we know as Kate and it will be there for you when you need it most."

She looked up, the muscles of her face slightly less drawn. "I'll try to remember that. Seems those are the memories we forget first."

"Like you, I am a survivor of multiple losses. I lost my brother, father, and mother in seventeen months. I'd like to ask you, what helped you survive? I learn a great deal from the answers I hear from others."

Kate sat very still, a puzzled expression replacing the sadness in her eyes. "I don't know," she mused. "There were so many different things that happened at the same time. It's hard to know just what did what." She let her conversation drift off, revisiting the painful past while I waited, certain I could see the wheels turning, scanning her memories.

"I am aware that losing a child is incredibly difficult. If you don't want to talk about it, I would understand." I had no desire to tip this beautiful caring daughter into despair. I needed her permission to talk about her pain.

"No, that's not it. I know it's good to talk about it. Right at the moment I just can't think what were the things that helped the most." Will moved near, as if to protect her, and mechanically she reached down and petted his head, lost in her memories of a tumultuous time.

Almost as an after thought, Kate offered, "There was one thing that was a turning point for me. Although, I don't remember realizing it at the time." Head tilted slightly, her eyes unfocused while remembering, she gingerly selected her words, searching for the correct order of events that had helped her.

"It was a time after I lost my son, and Mom had moved here to be with me. She felt I needed family, so she came to be near and help in any way she could. The five years she stayed really helped me. I was having such a rough time. I just couldn't get over Tom. Why did my little boy have to be taken from me? How could I go on?" She fiddled nervously with her coffee cup as she remembered the pain, her voice tight with the pressure of losing her child.

"I simply wasn't snapping out of it. People would ask me if I had accepted his death, or would tell me that in time I would learn to 'accept it.' That made me so angry! My feeling was no! No way! The word accept had the connotation of 'forgiveness,' even forgetting, and I just couldn't make myself feel I ever would or could accept his loss as even a little bit normal. I just knew my precious child I loved so much was gone and that was intolerable." Kate slumped at the memory, still able to impact her emotions after all these years.

"I remember telling Mom, people tell me, 'You just have to learn to accept it'. How can I accept it? How can I ever accept I had to lose my loving little boy? Can't people see how much they are asking of me?'

"I'll always remember what Mom told me. 'Well, there's other definitions for accept. It can mean other things. It can be an act of assimilating, taking in. For instance, think of a river. It just flows forward, knowing its job is to keep flowing. No matter what it finds in its path, the river follows its direction, and it just keeps going forward. Sometimes rocks fall into the river, even a boulder, but it accepts them and finds a way to keep going.'

"She told me I should think of my life as a river."

What wisdom, I thought.

My mind, alive with the metaphor and the amazing potential it held, glided easily through the vision I suddenly had of a vibrant, living river showing us the way. "It may have to change direction somewhat to continue, but it 'accepts' the obstacle. Like the river we must do what we were created to do," I said to myself.

"She made me realize that to accept something is not to say, 'Okay, all's well.' It really means to continue on, over, and around the obstacle and keep on going. I didn't realize it at the time, but that was a turning point for me."

"What a powerful message. Thank you for sharing that wonderful story with me. I am deeply moved by the hope in that message."

"I am certain Mom had no idea at the time how profoundly her interpretation of acceptance would help me. But it has helped me ever since, in some very important times."

It was a perfect moment for Margaret to wake up and join us at the table. "Kate has been sharing your wonderful story about the river accepting stones." A sleepy Margaret looked mystified.

"You remember, Mom, when I was having trouble accepting Tom's death, and you told me the story about the boulder in the river and learning acceptance?" she prompted. Slowly Margaret's quizzical face gave way to a smile of recognition and she nodded, her eyes watching Kate carefully.

"May I use your story to help others, Margaret?" I asked. "I know that it has the power to ease the pain for many, and it would please me if I could bring this to the wonderful people with whom I work."

She turned slowly in her chair to look at me, her face radiant with the sudden realization of her impact. "If you think it will help others, feel free to use it," she said.

We relived more moments of dealing with loss of many family members and felt the bond that shared experience creates. It is a strange club to belong to, this having experienced multiple losses. Not one of us would willingly apply for membership, I thought. Reluctantly, I brought our visit to a close after checking Margaret carefully, and finding no reason for changing our fairly smooth regimen. In spite of her need for increased sleep, she was maintaining strong vital signs that spoke volumes for her hearty constitution. I marveled at the strength she brought to her journey.

I pondered this as I drove to the next patient's. I was awash in rapidly tumbling emotions and realizations. Carefully I went over the story of the river in my mind, savoring it again and again, feeling the fresh lift of hope it brought. I said aloud, "This has been a priceless gift to me. I must find ways to share it with others, so they can experience the lift I just did."

It was not long before I had the opportunity to test the impact of this simple metaphor on others. It was my night to facilitate the support group where eight widows, who preferred to call themselves surviving spouses, honestly faced their sorrow and confronted together what might have seemed too much to do alone. "Tell me what your loss feels like," I led.

"Like the light in my life got really dim," said one.

"I wonder if I'll ever feel happy again."

"I just don't see how I'll ever get over it!"

The saddened faces of people who were grappling with the loss and searching for a way to move on looked back at me, their beseeching gaze a blend of resignation and unsettled need. It was the perfect moment to share the river analogy with them.

"I have just been told a beautiful story by one of my patients and I would like to share it with you. Would you like to hear it?" Eight nodding heads urged me forward.

As the story unfolded, I watched their body language. Slowly and carefully, I unfolded the story of the river and its purpose as faithfully as I could to Margaret's intent.

"How beautiful!"

"What a wonderful way to look at it."

"We are like the river, aren't we? We can choose to see it that way."

"The only choice we do have is to make it," volunteered one.

"You've got that right!" All eight voices spoke as one.

"That really has meaning for me. I guess we do have the task of finding our way forward, even if we can't picture it now. Thank her for us, will you, Joy?"

Back at Margaret's bedside I shared my experience with her. I saw the look of pleasure on her face as she realized her attempt to help Kate was now a vehicle for helping others. I thought, How many children this wonderful woman must have reached. She has such commitment to helping others.

To Margaret I said, "You must have been one heck of a teacher."

"Well, I certainly tried to reach them," she said modestly.

"With this story you'll go on reaching people. Thank you for letting me share your river story with others." I squeezed her hand and felt the moistness in my eyes. Looking over I saw her eyes were damp, too.

"Liquid love, that's what we have here," I said, while

laughing. "That's what tears are." Reaching over I gave her a warm hug and we patted each other's backs, sealing our moment of sharing with the endorsement a hug provides.

For Kate, as for all of us, knowing what she knew didn't stop the pain. Privately, while her mother was sleeping, I would say, "Let's talk about the pain, the incredible emotional pain of losing someone you love." It was something I tried to do with all my families.

"It's like you are caught in a swirling whirlpool of energy and can't get out," Kate answered. "There isn't any thought I can think, or anything I can do at any moment when I can forget, for even just a little bit, that I am losing someone I love."

Her explanation captured the moment succinctly. "Tell me about the pain, Kate."

"Sometimes I ask, why now? Why her? Even, why her and not me? One of the hardest parts of the pain is there are no answers to those questions. You're just left to wonder without any way to know," she said, while staring at the floor.

No two scenarios are the same. I knew that, with her major losses, she understood the stages of grief. What is not so obvious is that we can go through all the stages and bounce back and forth between them, sometimes in just ten minutes. For that matter, we can even experience more than one stage simultaneously. It's as if we've wandered into a foreign landscape, alien in every way, where our senses are both heightened and numbed at the same time. Even the colors and shapes around us assume different perspective, and we have no framework upon which we can neatly hang our understanding.

Grief knows no formula and each person must find her

own way through emotions, memories and feelings. All this flashed through my mind as I sought to comfort Kate.

"One thing I know for certain," I replied. "The pain is not a measure of how well or poorly you are doing. To do well handling grief is to still have pain. It's just that if you're doing well, you will find your way a little sooner." I watched Kate's mood shift as she let in those thoughts.

I looked for words that could have meaning. "The pain is a measure of how much you care, how much you love, how much you've lost, how much your life is changing. It is a measure of how profound is the impact on your daily schedule, the way you see your world, the way you see yourself. It's love that thinks it has no place to go."

She nodded, her face still sad and reflective, but her posture telegraphed to me she had begun to strengthen. "I just wish I felt I was doing a better job with Mom. It feels like I'm all thumbs or something."

"Nothing could be further from the truth!" I protested. "You are doing a wonderful job. Where is it written that you, and you alone, have to be perfect? I only wish others could see the creative approach you use. Most of all, I wish for you to be able to see for yourself the beauty of what you give."

We shared many times over the next few weeks, as the time felt right for talking.   Another day I said, "You know, part of what fuels us is to realize that whenever we are able to help someone, even just a little bit, to have an easier time with their own grief, then the loss we have experienced isn't a total waste. Otherwise, it feels like there was no point to it all. Do you know what I mean, Kate?"

Nodding she said, "I do, Joy. I just wish that what I had to give felt more meaningful. It doesn't feel enough." She was stating the classic dilemma of caregivers.

"You make every day as happy and meaningful as you can," I pointed out to her.

"I do try to do that," she admitted.

"The problem is, the best never feels good enough when we can't really change the final outcome. Your choice would be to turn it all around and have your mother's life go on. Because that can't happen, you question your best efforts are good enough. Well, that's simply not true."

"Do you really think so?" she asked.

"I know so! Your experience has shown you how precious the final moments are, and how precious they are all going to seem when your mother has died. Do you think that knowledge is pushing you to do even more?"

"You're probably right. I keep thinking I must do one thing or another, before it's too late. Maybe that is the pressure."

"Look at all the memories you are collecting for the future. I've really admired your approach. But it needs to be doable for you, Kate, in a way that is kind and supportive of your energy. I wonder if the trick here is to find a good balance between those two realizations."

"You're right about that. I do know how much it will all mean and I keep thinking I'll be wishing I had done this or remembered something really important I am now forgetting. It's like I'll be losing a precious piece of what we've had together, with no way to get it back. I'm not concerned about me, right now, and I have to admit, there's not much balance in that."

"We have a saying in home care. Take care of the caregiver or pretty soon everyone's a patient." I smiled at her, knowing well the pressure she was feeling.

Kate chuckled. "I can see what you mean."

"There's one more point I want to share. You sound like you are having a good case of the 'if onlys,' as I call it. We all find ourselves saying, if only this hadn't happened, or if only this could happen. I have found feeling 'if only' to be one of the stages of grief we can't avoid, only it's not a stage very often identified. We feel blindsided by it and quickly become overwhelmed when it arrives as if on cue."

Kate nodded. "I guess I wish I could change everything for my mom like she did for me. If only I could give her new life, like learning to accept from her viewpoint gave me new life."

Nodding, I understood this was at the heart of her sorrow. "There is nothing anyone can do more than their very best at the moment. It becomes imperative that we know this, see it, and honor that in ourselves. You are changing everything for her in so many ways. It is too soon to be able to add up all that you do and you are making a very significant difference in your mother's life." Kate nodded her head as I spoke, and I watched her whole body reverberate with the truth she acknowledged.

It's such a long process, this business of accepting the unacceptable and moving on, I thought.

Eventually Margaret's condition worsened. She was obviously much weaker. Vital signs, that barometer of so much in human change, began to shift from her normal values. Increased pain was now an issue for me to address and I changed the frequency of my visits. At times I would arrive to find her in too much pain, the current dosage of her medication no longer working. I would call the doctor, get a new order for increased medication, and teach Margaret and Kate the new schedule. Then for a time Margaret would move back into comfortable days, until the growth of her cancer caused the pain to escalate once more and we repeated the procedure. Kate went right on making every day count in magical ways, staying close to her mom while keeping busy on days when her mother only needed to sleep.

Some days we returned to the comfortable laughter that had been our norm. Those days we continued to share our magical moments, silently feeling grateful for the blessing of another good day.

"I've had a good life," Margaret said. "I'm so glad I did all the things I did while I could." There were never complaints. She simply became quiet and reserved when days were not up to the former speed and vigor she had managed for so long.

Her family came in from around the country to say their good-byes and to share her ebullient spirit. Once more Kate followed her impeccable instincts and let others know now would be a good time to visit, before it was too late to say the things that needed to be said. "Finishing the unfinished business is important," she said. Will kept closer guard at Margaret's side, so we all sensed she was likely preparing to say good-bye to us sooner than we had hoped.

Kate continued to busy herself with projects. Now she was decorating sweatshirts for Christmas presents and her keen sense of color, imagination, and creativity combined to produce inviting gifts for others. How wise she is, I thought. Margaret isn't well enough to do things, but Kate senses she must continue to use her creativity to balance her own day and energies. She has learned so much about how to go forward.

With honesty Kate faced the not so good moments of self-doubt I hear at every bedside. "I just hope I'll know what to do when the moment comes."

"You only have to call and we'll be able to give you advice over the phone, or we'll come over and assist you with knowing what to do." I tried to reassure her. "That's always possible, twenty-four hours a day."

Some patients, sensing that time is running out, want constant and closer companionship with a loved one near. Some withdraw emotionally to prepare for their deaths, moving into a very private realm with few words spoken, and even less clues given for what they are feeling. Margaret chose the latter route.

"She just told me, 'I need to be alone to do this myself'. I have to honor that." Kate's instincts when to honor and when to intervene were top notch. I also respected Margaret's choice and I tried not to interrupt unnecessarily as I checked her pain level and listened to her lungs, to be certain she did not develop pneumonia from being in bed all the time, as now the weakness made it impossible for her to be upright.

"I realize you want to be alone most of the time, Margaret, and I want to respect that. Can we establish a system where I'll ask you each visit if there's anything we need to check, and have you know that's your signal to clue me you need to talk?"

Margaret nodded in agreement. "It's just so hard to talk now, and my mind seems to be somewhere else."

I understood what she meant. Her elsewhere mind was dealing with the mental and spiritual aspects of dying. As briefly as was possible, I shared with her an understanding of the work that must happen on other dimensions as we prepare to move on. On the days she had more energy and could talk, I would relate some small nugget of understanding about the process she was in, that I hoped would help her without intruding on her solitary journey.

"Do you see the white light yet?" I asked on one visit.

"I think so, but it's quite far away." There was no missing her weakness as she spoke.

"We've talked about it before, Margaret, but it's worth saying again. It'll be beautiful and full of love, so let it happen naturally, as you are, without worrying about it. The distance just means it isn't quite time." Her brief nod assured me she was remembering our preparation for this time.

Out in the kitchen I talked with Kate. "I've often wondered why some people withdraw this much. Clearly Margaret feels the need to spend time by herself. It will be nice if someday we know for certain all the reasons why that happens. What I do know is she's doing work on many levels—emotionally, spiritually, and mentally as well as physically. With little energy it becomes imperative to give that energy over to the work at hand." I paused, searching for how to capture with simple words the process we were seeing.

"One thing I do understand. The soul is in charge. We must remember there are reasons even if we, in our limited views cannot see them. The soul got her this far and we can trust it now."

Kate continued on her path, giving loving care, while balancing her own needs with her mother's need to spend time alone. On a day when Margaret felt a sudden burst of energy, I was able to tell her, once more, how much she meant to me.

"I'll never forget you, Margaret. Thanks for being in my life. I can't overstate what a gift your presence has been to me," I told her, looking into her eyes.

She smiled serenely, voice nearly gone, and nodded ever so briefly, her bright eyes holding mine in wordless appreciation. In the end, as most often happens, Margaret died peacefully at the time her soul and body chose for her, as she had wished in her daughter's home. I went to see Kate as soon as the phone call came.

When I entered the home I could see evidences of Kate's strength, and as I had predicted, she was able to do everything necessary. "Mom continued to need to be alone and I just kept going into her room every now and then to be certain she didn't need anything," she told me. "I heard her breathing change in the early morning hours, over the baby monitor we had set up, and then I stayed a little closer. But I still tried to honor that request to be alone." She was calm and peaceful as she relayed the end, and her complete respect for her mother's need to finish living in the way she chose.

"I don't think she was really alone. Although I couldn't really hear anything she was saying, it felt like she was communicating with others. She was very busy looking around as if listening to something, or to someone. Finally she just took one last breath, and didn't breathe again." Kate relaxed into a gentle smile as she added up what she had witnessed. "I'm going to really miss her, but at least I know I let her do it the way she wanted to. And that helps."

"There is no greater gift we give to others than to let them have their choices to follow their own paths, Kate. That was a wonderful way to honor your mother."

I looked around and saw a lifeless looking St. Bernard, flat on his stomach, paws outstretched to hold his forlorn looking head. "How is Will doing?"

"He just lay outside her door and waited, too. You can tell he is missing her." She reached down and petted the head of the St. Bernard who was looking at her with doleful eyes.

"Don't ever let your pain keep you from realizing the wonderful job you have done and are doing, Kate. You are in pain and you are doing beautifully. One doesn't cancel out the other."

In the days ahead I kept in touch with Kate via phone. She was gone for several days while they took Margaret home to the Bronx for burial beside the husband and daughter already there. A few weeks later I stopped back to see her in person. Will met me at the door and Kate invited me into her dining room.

"Kate, I am so grateful for you and your mother in my life. You have done so well. Not only are you such a sterling example of a caring daughter, but also your open sharing with me has really enriched my life. I am especially grateful for the gift of the river and its acceptance. But I have one request."

Kate looked at me thoughtfully. "What is it, Joy?"

"I would like permission to share your mother's story and the circumstances of all her losses when I share her story of the river. She really deserves credit for it, Kate. And you deserve credit for the wonderful gifts of healing and tender beauty you brought to the sadness. Others need to know that beautiful sadness is possible in the heart of our grief. Would you mind?"

Kate's face registered her excitement. "Oh, Joy! I think that would be wonderful. Mom would be very pleased."

We hugged. "Thank you, Kate. I am grateful for that. From now on I will share with all who hear her story of the river that it came from a woman with a wonderful mind, who brought her indomitable spirit and marvelous creativity to the task of facing grief. We are all richer from being touched by that spirit. I'll never forget her. I'll never forget what she taught me about how to accept the unacceptable. I'll never forget your wonderful part in this story too, Kate."

We reached across the table and joined hands. "And yours too, Will!" The big St. Bernard wagged his tail and then settled back at our feet, to help us reminisce about his friend.

Moving On

Life can only be understood backwards, but it must be lived forwards.

~ Soren Kierkegaard

The warm breeze, wafting its way among the buildings of brick and stone on the picturesque campus, seemed to welcome and reassure me. I felt the wind's gentle caress and experienced another wave of excitement for the moment about to unfold. I had been invited to share some of my writing about dying at a small intimate conference in the Midwest. The experience was both thrilling and scary.

What would it be like to hear my own words aloud and to see the response? I am used to talking from the heart with people, who are in various stages or aspects of dealing with grief. Now one more step was being taken. All the while I recognized the hand of fate was nudging me forward, I recognized the familiar feeling of cold feet. Soon I would know what I had come here to know: the response of caring, thoughtful people to my preliminary writing for a book.

I entered the room where I would share what I had been learning, in one way or another, for many years, and reflected on the journey. It had been a long path from losing so many of my family in my early thirties to this moment that welcomed me now. I need not have worried.

"I can't wait to read it!"

"That was so moving, to hear your stories of people facing grief."

"You must finish this book and publish it!"

Strolling across campus now, on the way to my dormitory, I was joined by Ingrid, who had been in one of the sessions. "I would like to share my story with you," she began. Her words were laced with a German accent and she spoke hesitantly, waiting for my permission. "In the class, I told a little bit about when my two adult sons made their transition, just four months apart. Now I would like to share more with you, if you are willing to listen."

"Oh, indeed I am. That must have been so difficult!" I turned toward her keenly aware of the privilege it is to share life's important moments with another.

"Like you, I studied with Elizabeth Kubler Ross, and that helped me a great deal. She was an excellent teacher and a great comfort in my time of sorrow. I don't know what I would have done without the information I learned from her; it helped me so much!" she said.

"I am so glad you found her. She truly changed the nature of grieving for the world. Tell me more about your sons." I reached over and touched Ingrid's back with my hand, as we moved slowly along the tree-lined walk. The gentle breeze caressed our faces, and I noticed we had fallen into step with each other.

"Losing two sons in four months was the most difficult time I have ever faced in this life. Allen worked in commercial oil drilling in the Gulf Coast. He and one of his crew lost their lives in a severe storm, when something went wrong and they were swept overboard from the rig when it broke from the heavy winds and rain. No trace was ever found of either of them after the storm that night. Just like that, pouf, he was gone.

"Only four months after Allen's death, my oldest son, John, lost his life in an automobile accident near New York City. The phone call came early the next morning and just like that, he too was gone without my having any real understanding of what had happened."

"How awful! I can't imagine facing that." I experienced the stab of pain felt mother-to-mother and stopped walking. Dear God, how does anyone lose their children? Not just one, but two sons, I thought. Losing a child is every parent's nightmare, and she lost two just four months apart. I looked into her face, which showed controlled sadness creating a mask-like expression, hiding all but the pain in her eyes.

"I have seen my sons in my dreams many times since they died and I have come to feel the dreams and messages from them are like postcards they sent me," she said.

"Postcards from the other side. What a wonderful way to look at it."

"They tell me that they are happy and well, and what a comfort it is to hear that. I believe we need to share that this happens, so others will open up to the possibilities. Somehow I got the feeling you believe these things can happen also." She glanced at me, no doubt wondering if she had misjudged my openness to such a topic.

"Yes, I really do," I said. "Sometimes I think about putting a chapter into my book called The Wild, The Wonderful, And The Improbable. Not everyone sees these things as valid or believable, but I guess what I care most about, is that others get a chance to decide for themselves."

"It's surprising how many feel they, too, have these experiences, once we open up and talk about it," she said.

We found a low stone wall and sat down, swinging our legs casually, in stark contrast to the highly serious topic we shared. "Tell me more about how it was for you."

"When Allen drowned at sea, one of the things that haunted me was that I would not see him anymore. No trace of them ever found and we had no body to bury. I found myself talking to my son, telling him I could not bear that I would not see him again. Four days later, I saw Allen in a dream. It was a spiritual dream, or a dream with a message. I don't know what to call it. Allen was in my bedroom pointing to a drawer in my dresser. He wanted me to see something. Then he was gone. As I awoke, I went to the dresser drawer and opened it, attempting to see what it was he wanted me to find. I noticed a movie reel of him when he was little and suddenly knew he was telling me I could still see him in the home movies we had taken." Her face brightened recalling the poignant moment that held so much healing for her grief.

"How comforting that must have been. Did seeing the movies help?"

"Oh, yes! It helped me know I still had something I could hang on to. I believe my son is fine, that where he has gone, he is in peace and joy. It was that I needed something to reach out and touch. The way his death happened, the funeral and wake and all the things which usually help death be more real, were not possible." Regret once more filled her expression and one lone jaw muscle tightened as if in protest against the unthinkable which still tugged at her heart.

I reflected on her words. "It's hard to believe what a helping factor a funeral can be, until we go through one for

someone we really love. Then we see that time as an opportunity for learning we must accept the unacceptable, and a
time for getting used to the way it's going to be with the
love and help of those around us."

"Support, from the people who are most important to us
holds us together.   Although people were wonderful, there
was no finish to it," she stated.

"I understand. Have you had other dreams of Allen?"

"Many. I can't remember them all at the moment, but
they have been messages of encouragement. For instance, I
had a dream in which Allen and I were together. He was but
a small boy again and he pointed to his shoes, which were
navy and white tennis shoes. Later, I had to think much
about this, and then I realized. It was a message. 'Mom,
remember the nice dark navy and white Italian shoes you
brought me from Europe?' I felt he wanted me to remember the joy he had when he was here, and he wanted me to
feel good about the things I had done for and with him,
things that had been special to him.

"You know, Joy, I would like to encourage parents to keep
in mind that we can still talk to our children after they are
gone. They can hear us so, we can speak to them of how
much we love them. We send our thoughts like postcards to
them. They can get back to us if we let them. I believe we
stay connected like we are one."

"Ingrid, I think that's a very important message. The stories I hear from near-death survivors have convinced me
that people who die know our thoughts and hear our
words. To go ahead and say what we need to say is a big help
to us when we're grieving."

"It helped me to know I had something I could still do.
That's so important. And with Allen, there were no arrange-

ments to make, no last times to say good-bye in person, no
way to reach out and touch him. With John I could do that,
and those things helped." Her hands moved busily in the air,
as if even now she needed to do something at the thought
of having been robbed of those precious moments with
Allen.

We resumed walking in silence, each lost in our own
thoughts for a moment. Then hesitating slightly, she said,
"There's more. Do you want to hear it?"

"Please go on."

"I was born and raised in Germany and I have friends and
family there. It helped to have a few open-minded friends
and family members to tell about my feelings and experiences that are called intuitive or knowing. I feel blessed. I
believe everyone can and does have these experiences, and
when we allow ourselves to open to them and work with
them, we can be prepared for what is ahead." She reached
up and stroked her cheek lightly, remembering the painful
time she had been through.

"I have believed in angels and helpers as long as I can
remember," she continued. "When I think back, I am certain I had some warnings before my sons died that helped
prepare me. The summer before their deaths, my youngest
daughter gave us two wall pictures as an anniversary present.
The frames were brown, with matted pictures that had a
black border around them. My daughter could not have
known that in Germany, a death announcement always has
a black frame around the paper and envelope. They looked
to me like two death announcements and I became sad
every time I looked at them. In fact, I could not bear to
hang them on a wall and put them away in a drawer. In
February, I developed a feeling that someone in uniform

would come to my house and tell me about my son. I kept having those feelings all month.

"The Gulf War was going on, and I knew that when a member of our military died, someone in uniform goes to the home of that person to inform the family. I thought, Well, this cannot be for me. Allen is on an oil rig; John is in New York City. Neither of them is in the military, so this must be what others are experiencing who have children in the service. Perhaps I am picking up on them. But the feeling was still there. At the end of March, a local sheriff in uniform came to my house to inform me that my son, Allen, was missing at sea. The Coast Guard had asked the police department to let the family know.

"I had known in my heart this was coming. Still, shock waves washed over my body." I stopped walking and reached for her hand, needing to reach out and touch her.

"How soon did you make the connection with your feeling?"

"I think it came to me quite quickly. Most importantly, I no longer had that feeling. In fact, I've never had it since."

"That speaks for itself, doesn't it? Were you warned about John's death, too?" I asked.

"On the day John died—which was four months later—my husband and I had gone to the river to see about picking wild black raspberries to make jelly. When we got to the place, I felt a heaviness, a sadness. Something was going to happen. I could not see a picture in my mind of what it meant. I tried to push it away, think of other things. When we got home, the whole house was sad. I could 'see' dark shadows. It was awful! 'Keep yourself busy,' I said to myself. So I made jelly and cooked supper and tried to fill the time with good activity.

"The next morning I received a phone call that John, my oldest son, lost his life the night before in an automobile accident." Although her face remained calm and serene, Ingrid's eyes clouded once more with pain as she remembered. "It took several days for the body to be brought back to our town for the funeral. When he was home, I was praying the Rosary beside his body. During my prayer I 'saw' the latest photo I had of John and me, coming toward me. It was being held by an unseen someone. As the picture came closer, I was asked in thought if I would like to get back into the church again. As a divorced and remarried Catholic, I could not take communion and had stopped going to church. Suddenly I realized how much I had missed that. I knew instantly that I didn't need to feel guilty. Just make a choice to return. After the funeral, I was asked to join the Catholic church by someone from the congregation. It just felt like John had it all arranged for me."

I squeezed her hand, excited at the importance of all this for her. "I've had visits in dreams with him," she continued. "It is very comforting. In one dream both Allen and John came to visit. It was a dream I'll never forget!" Her radiant smiling face told me something very healing had happened. I asked myself, "What could have happened here that made so much difference?"

"John brought Allen to me and both were very much alive. We hugged, and when they left, I could feel the love from their hearts to my heart. It felt like warm electrical waves."

There was no doubting her sincerity. She was willing to share her story to help others and had courageously opened her heart to me, a relative stranger, with only the hope that others would not feel as much pain from their own loss if they knew what she had experienced. The absolute change in her feelings to ones of peace was a testimony to the validity of her experiences.

"Ingrid, if I can find the way to write it, would you consent to let this be in my book? I agree that it's time people heard these things. There's so much potential comfort if people feel these events are normal enough to trust them."

"I'd be honored. I am pleased you understand," she replied.

"You seem to have dealt with your grief very well, and I admire what you have achieved. Did you always believe that death was peaceful?" I asked.

"As a small child, I nearly drowned, became unconscious and had to be brought back to life. There was no pain, I felt warm and had no fear. I've thought a lot about that, and I think I had the experience of nearly drowning so I would know there is no pain to death. It prepared me for what happened later."

Another near-death experience that changed a life ahead for the better, I thought.

"Now, in prayer and thoughts, I send love to my sons and I'm sure this reaches them. They send love in return, and I feel the warmth. I believe we don't lose our loved ones. They are there to greet us when we make our transition. The love we give and share will always be with us. When we pass into the next plane of life, we are alive in a new place. But we still can communicate. We can send postcards with our thoughts." Ingrid's face had transcended the pain; her eyes relaxed and now a gentle smile signaled the resolution of her heart and mind working in tandem at last.

"I love your point of view. I feel we really just have a new address in the cosmos." I gave her an exuberant hug, and happily we resumed walking along our path to the dormitory.

"As a nurse, have you heard similar stories?" she asked.

"Many times. Patients often feel free to talk to nurses about their innermost thoughts and experiences. Some have told me about premonitions they had, which happened later on, just as they saw them. They talked about seeing or hearing someone who had died, and just knew it was real. Some have relatives who had near death experiences, or had experienced a near-death experience themselves. All of these carried the common theme that it changed for the better the way these people handled their situations. To witness that, I couldn't help believing something significant had occurred."

"You have been in an ideal spot to see this, Joy."

"You are so right. Maybe if I hadn't become a nurse I couldn't believe as easily as I do, but the many different experiences I have heard over the years, not just recently, have brought me to the conclusion there is much more happening at death, and in life, than we realize."

"I feel that the way I received help with my grief is open to others. If only others can trust enough to let themselves be open they will find help also." Her face and eyes were bright with conviction.

"Maybe now, with all the talk about angels, people are ready to believe."

Laughing young adults were playing an impromptu game of soccer on the green and our attention drifted to the fun they had created. You are living in a different world than we did, I thought. Wonder if we'll do a better job of teaching you about death than we received?

"Joy," she asked, "have you also had dreams of your loved ones?" Her question focused my attention once more.

"Yes, I have. My mother died two days after I had taken over the care of my mother-in-law, whom we had found on the floor. We created an apartment in our walkout basement, one where she would not fall down stairs as she was legally blind and could not see danger. She had dementia and could not accurately tell me how she felt, or what she needed. My mother would come to me in a dream occasionally and say, 'It's time to go clean the cellar' as if we were to go down together and clean. I would awaken, and go downstairs to check on my mother-in-law. I always found she was ill or in need of something."

Ingrid laughed a delighted and understanding laugh.

"The dream only came when there was something wrong. Although it only happened a handful of times, if I had the recurring dream I would get up and go check. Sure enough, something was needed. It's really quite an efficient message service." Our laughing eyes met, comfortable enough with our subject to see the humor.

"I was struck by your heaviness on the day John died," I went on. "My brother was killed in a helicopter crash just after lunch time. I had put my little one down for a nap and suddenly felt exhausted, all in. It was such a sudden weariness, and that surprised me. I decided to nap while my son slept. I couldn't sleep, and while I was trying to, the phone rang with the news my brother had been killed instantly. I've always felt that on some level those two incidents were connected."

"Yes, that is close to what I felt. An all-over heaviness that makes you feel you can't go on," she said.

"For years I wondered about that. Somewhere I read that we exchange energies when we have relationships with others, and when someone we really love dies, they give us back our energy and take back their own. That made sense to me," I said.

"I never thought about it like that but it makes sense to me, too."

"It seems to explain why we feel so empty and restless at the same time. Empty, because we have given back, to the one who died, the energy we had of theirs, and restless, because we have some energy of our own back to reinvest. Probably that is why keeping busy helps, at least temporarily and in a limited way. We reinvest some of our energy and have additional energy to add to our own. Essentially I believe we have to rearrange our energy when someone we love deeply dies." Dodging the cracks in the sidewalk, we turned the corner and started up the circular walkway to the front door.

The clock in the campus tower tolled the hour, the melodious chimes telling us what our stomachs knew: Time for dinner. We had arrived at our destination. "Ingrid, if you have had other experiences I would enjoy hearing them. Do you think you could write them down and send them to me?"

"I'd be glad to. I'll have to think about them; there have been so many."

Our special time of sharing was sealed with another hug. We exchanged addresses and went our separate ways. There's a unique bond that happens between people who have experienced death of their loved ones, I thought. Maybe it's that you don't have to explain the dicey moments. The shared pain gives you an automatic place of acceptance, just as you are. It feels so good to know there are others who can hear about the pain and understand.

The conference came to an end after lunch the next day, and we traded the serenity of a spacious tree-lined campus with gracious stone buildings, for the utilitarian concrete of an airport with its bucket seats. There I found Ingrid waiting for the same plane to Chicago. I watched her intently as she stood in the check-in line. To look at this joyous, kindly grandmother, there was no way to tell she had been through such profound loss. "Clearly she has moved through her loss and been uplifted by her experience in a way that can't be missed," I said to myself. "How do we let people know this kind of peace is possible when we stay open to new understanding? I want to find that way!"

The Sunday afternoon crowd bustled noisily around us, impatiently waiting for the moment to be on the way again. We found seats together in the lounge where we could continue to talk, after laughing at the coincidence that had us talking again. I looked into her eyes and saw that they sparkled with life, the zest she felt for living there for all to see.

"Tell me more about your experiences, Joy. This gives me a chance to hear more of your stories."

"My father died, just five months after my brother. I woke up in the night to hear our dog, with her puppies in the garage, howling loudly. Funny thing is, this dog never howled. I can't remember ever hearing her do it before or since. I was thinking about getting up to check on the puppies, wondering if something was threatening them, when the phone rang. My father had just had a heart attack and was on his way to the hospital in an ambulance, which had left five minutes earlier. I got dressed and checked quickly on the puppies. I couldn't see anything wrong. I drove to the hospital only to find my father had not arrived.

"I called home and found that he died in the ambulance, about two miles from home, although my sister-in-law was unaware of that when she called me. Since I had glanced at the clock when the dog began howling and knew the time, I realized it was the very moment my father must have died." Ingrid nodded vigorously, not at all surprised.

"Have you felt the presence of any of your family after they died?" She glanced at her watch. "We have time to talk and I'd like to hear your experiences. That's one dividend from getting to the airport early."

"When my mother died, I felt especially grief stricken, as I had been scheduled to visit her on the day my mother-in-law became ill. I had rescheduled my visit for two days later, the day she died, only to end up canceling it, because I still needed to care for my ailing mother-in-law. I called her late in the morning to tell her I couldn't come that day either. It turned out I was the last person to talk to her. You can imagine how badly I felt!"

"Oh, yes. And guilty too, probably," Ingrid nodded, in agreement.

"Very guilty! My parents lived on a farm, and before my father died, we had promised both parents we would follow their wishes and have their funerals in the farmhouse. I didn't want to leave my mother alone before the funeral, so I stayed the first night in the house, along with an aunt who wouldn't hear of me staying there by myself.

"I went in by the casket and was crying, feeling so badly and in my mind saying, 'Do you know how badly I feel, Mother? How I let you down?' Well, I heard back the answer, 'Of course I do and it's all right. I'm fine. You just did what you had to do.' Then I felt the feeling you only get when your mother comforts you. It was as if she had wrapped me in her arms and made it feel all right again. You know, no one else has the same feeling as a mother, no matter how sincere the caring."

"No one else," she agreed.

"When it was as if I could feel her arms were around me, do you know what happened? I suddenly felt peace. Still sad, and missing her, but with a difference only her caring understanding could have provided. I feel it was one of your knowings, Ingrid."

"How beautiful! A postcard from the other side." Ingrid beamed at me. "Does this ever happen from those you take care of after they die, Joy?"

"From time to time. Sometimes, while I am meditating, the face of a patient who died will pass before my eyes and wave, smiling. It doesn't seem to be anything I have any control over. At times I feel a tingle or buzzing in some place on my head, feel the person as if present with me. No two people seem to buzz the same place." I laughed. "I feel they are letting me know they are doing fine."

"That's the message." We chuckled in unison, each happy to share her view with a kindred spirit who didn't feel this was the least bit unusual.

"Just recently I had a special patient, very ill, who fought gallantly, with one of the most exceptional spirits I have ever seen, in spite of the very severe diseases she had. We talked about death, but Dorothy was so invested in living fully every minute, I knew she wasn't really focusing on dying, even though she listened to my point of view. She went into the hospital in the middle of the night, and just hours later, she was gone. I came home the next day to the message on my answering machine that she had died."

"What did you do?" Ingrid's face clouded with caring for the shock I had felt, recognizing what it is like to experience the feelings of death without any warning.

"I sat down, feeling so badly, for I really loved this lady and she me. She had told me I felt like the sister she never had. The last time I saw her she said, 'Good-bye, Sis. I love you.' As I sat there, remembering this, really missing her and feeling so sad, it was as if her presence entered the room. I could feel her near for a few minutes, and there was a warmth of great love and joy. It's the only way I can describe it. As if she were finding a way to comfort me and reassure me she was fine."

"Yes." Ingrid nodded. "That's just how I've felt it, too."

"After that I was still sad, but definitely all right again. It's funny…how remembering these moments brings back the peace and joy." Glancing sideways I saw Ingrid's delighted smile. I figured she must have been happy to be remembering her special moments with someone who thought like she did. "You know, you can't tell these things to everyone. People are quick to judge and I always get the feeling someone will want to drop a net over us and cart us away!" We laughed, both of us familiar with the disbelief of others. We had stopped talking, the moment accentuated by our pause, highlighting how we had met in the middle of our very dissimilar lives at the crossroads of shared experiences.

"I know what you mean. Some of my friends can handle this and some can't. Lately, though, I think more people are ready for hearing these stories. I'll tell you one thing: It has certainly made me look at life with a more open mind. And I'll always be grateful for how it helped me handle losing my sons."

As she spoke, the harsh blaring sound of the boarding announcement let us know we were ready to get on our plane. Reluctantly, we returned to dealing with the logistics of the present and moved into the line, patiently enduring the press of travelers eager to get home after an eventful weekend. So intent were we on our topic, I barely felt the aggravation of pushing people, usually a part of traveling I dreaded. We said good-bye to each other at the door to the plane and moved to our separate seats for the journey home. "Wonder what the future will bring for us both and what 'postcards' we'll have for each other in the years ahead?" I asked myself as I sat in my seat and buckled my seat belt.

Little more than a month later her letter arrived. "I have been thinking of you and wanted to write to you sooner. Then my darling little grandson thought I was a monkey bar at the playground, hung on my arms, the rest you can imagine. My arm is well enough now to write as I promised.

"Would like to share with you some of the knowing I had before my grandmother, mother and my two sons made their transitions. What we call 'death'. Of course you and I know there is no death and I hope that someday soon everyone knows this, too.

"My 'helpers' have been wonderful. They have showed me in symbolic dreams, thoughts, etc. that someone in my family would soon die. I'll pick out the best ones to tell you.

"The day my grandmother died, I had a dream and in the dream I saw a church with an old fashioned black hearse and horses standing by. The coachman, who sat on the seat up on the hearse and held a whip in his hand, turned his face toward me and nodded 'yes'. When I awoke, I knew that my grandmother had just died in Germany. I woke up my husband to tell him.

"At one p.m. that day I received an overseas telegram stating that my grandmother had died in Germany, giving the date and the time. When I figured the time difference I found it would have been just about the time I was dreaming about her.

"When my mother died, again I knew ahead of time. I was in the front of our home here in the States. The evergreen tree in the front yard gave out a fragrance that reminded me of German cemeteries. This was how I interpreted it. Then I said, "*Morsuleum.*" That is the German word and I wondered why I said that and couldn't explain this even to myself. My mother's birthday was approaching, and I had a gift for her ready to be mailed and felt that this was not necessary, that mom did not need anything.

"Shortly after that, I received a phone call from my sister stating our mother had died of a massive heart attack.

"Two weeks later, as I was driving in traffic and stopped at a red light, I could smell violets, lots of violets. (Have to mention here that the violets have a very nice fragrance in Europe, but the same violets here do not have this fragrance. Nevertheless, that was the very fragrance I smelled.)

"That evening as I was visiting with some friends at a home of one of them, there was a vase and I felt I had to really study the paintings on the vase. There were violets on the vase. I thought about the fragrance I had smelled that afternoon and mentioned it to my friends.

"Two weeks later I received a large box from my sister from overseas. In the box was our mom's china with violets, all neatly wrapped in gift paper. Mom had mentioned at one time to my sister that if anything ever happened to her, she should send her china to me."

The letter went on to confirm the details of the experiences that preceded her sons' deaths she had shared on our campus walk. I felt once more the impact of our time together. She concluded with, "Dear Joy. Hope you can read this. Had I written it all in the German language it would be more colorful. Take care and keep in touch. Thanks! Love and Blessings, Ingrid."

From time to time we talk on the phone, as she lives in the Midwest, I in the East. In a recent conversation I asked, "Tell me, Ingrid, do you still see your sons in your dreams?"

"Oh, yes. Not as often. But it's beautiful when it happens. Just recently my oldest son, John, was there as he was as a little child, right before we moved to the States. We were staying with my grandmother, as my husband had gone before us to find work and a place to live. The dream was a beautiful scene from that time, and when I woke up the whole room was filled with love. I was quite exhilarated for several days."

"How wonderful! A postcard of love. You were right about something else, Ingrid."

"Oh, what's that?"

"People are getting ready to talk about these things. More and more of my patients and their families are willing to discuss such happenings, and almost every family has a story to tell. It's really quite exciting to be a hospice nurse these days! Promise me one thing, Ingrid."

"What's that, Joy?

"You'll keep on letting me in on these events. You know I'm fascinated. Although I hope there are no more tragedies for you to endure, keep sending me the stories you remember of your knowings."

"It's a deal, Joy, if you'll promise one thing to me."

"What's that?" I wondered what the gentle and generous Ingrid could want.

"That we'll talk in ten years time about this and see how far the public has come in accepting what you and I have come to see as so natural. It should be one very exciting conversation, reviewing all the changes."

"Ingrid, you have a deal!"

My Time, My Turn

Tragedy is a tool for the living to gain wisdom, not a guide by which to live.

~ Robert Kennedy

The day was seemingly perfect. Golden sunlight streaked across the gently rolling waves that were pursuing their persistent search for the shore. The bright and friendly sun was high in the sky overhead warming the day and my heart. Lazy seagulls soared and dove toward the beach, reflecting how carefree and joyous I felt.

I had been writing most of the day. Now I strolled along the streets of Laguna Beach on my customary break, reflecting on how wonderful it felt to be revisiting the meaningful times I had shared with my patients. As I wrote down stories of their growth I noted the magical gifts of understanding they had given me, and the memories nourished my inner self once again.

I swung into the bakery and bought a cookie and a cool drink, then sat on the bench outside and soaked up the ambience of easy living with sunshine, warmth, and cheerful sounds all around. Cookies are my comfort food from early childhood years. They speak of love and ease, of pampering myself, and saying all is well in my world.

By now the streets had a familiar ring from the several weeks I had strolled them between long hours of remembering special people, moments and happenings in their lives, now immortalized in written words. The emerging stories that held such power for me had brought my writing journey this far. I felt happy, energized, and incredibly grateful as I relived the special time and moments shared with people I recognized had been an immense gift to my life.

It was an undeniable privilege to share another's life as he or she is preparing to die.

I felt alive with the realization of the many gifts my special patients had provided.

I lazily strode down the sloping hill, rounded the corner, and walked the last two blocks to my temporary residence. The thirty steps to my basement studio apartment, covered with a flowering canopy of lush California foliage, had the feel of a cathedral archway to me. I swung jauntily through and down the stairs with a song in my heart.

How odd, I thought. There is a note on my door. I wonder who could have left it as hardly anyone knows I am here.

No moment of anxiety or feeling of trepidation entered me as I read the words telling me my daughter had called and wished me to call her back. My neighbor, whose emergency phone number I had left with my children just in case, had received the message and invited me to come upstairs and use her phone to return the call. It was with mild curiosity I did so, using my phone card to call Canada.

"Hi, Mom. How is everything with you? Fine, I hope."

"I'm great, Ellen. It is a beautiful day here, and I'm having a wonderful time writing. What's up with you?"

"Well, unfortunately I have some bad news for you. I received a call from Pierre's daughter, Jan, telling me he died last night from a massive coronary. She wanted you to know. I'm really sorry, Mom. I realize you recently broke your engagement, but I know this must be a shock for you."

Pierre was dead. My brain didn't want to wrap around the unimaginable for a moment, as if my response was suddenly flat-lined. My brain went into overdrive. Pierre dead? Healthy Pierre who had just had a physical and was pronounced in unbelievably good health? How could that be, out of the blue like this.

"What happened? Do you know?"

"Only that he returned from a short business and pleasure trip, had flown in a glider the day before he returned home, and was home a short time when he went to visit a neighbor in his building. He died suddenly, the neighbor gave him CPR, and he went to the hospital. He didn't make it, Mom. They couldn't bring him back. Are you all right?"

"I think so. It certainly is shocking, and I'm sorry you had to be the bearer of such bad news. Thanks so much for letting me know." My words had a distant sound to my ears, a disconnect from the full impact of what we were discussing that momentarily held back full realization of the words just spoken.

We discussed the possibilities as one by one we tackled the questions: What do you think you will do now, Mom? Can I do anything to help? Do you think you want to come home for the funeral? Do you know yet what you wish to do?

We agreed Ellen would let Jan know she had reached me.
I wrote down Jan's phone number. "Tell her I'll call her later
this evening and try to talk with her. One way or another
I'll be in touch."

"Let me know how you are, Mom, and what you decide
to do. I'll help in any way I can." Her reassuring calm and
gentle support had cushioned the shock as much as was possible. I hung up the phone feeling nourished by her genuine
caring.

I walked back down the steps, this time unaware of the
growing splendor overhead, out of touch with the breath-
taking view of the ocean and beach, numbed and trying to
make sense of it all. I was going through the motions of
returning to my apartment. My mind reeled. Pierre gone.
"It was just a few weeks ago, when we understood our
engagement wasn't going to work out the way we had
hoped and broke the bond. Gone. Now you're gone. Just
like that. I just had the second letter from you, and we were
going to meet again when I returned. Pierre, how did this
happen? You left before we could talk once more, and
now…" I talked to him in my mind, thoughts tumbling one
upon another.

I reached the door and fumbled with the lock, sticky at
best of moments, now clearly adding to the feeling of confusion sweeping over me. I entered the apartment searching
for what to do next. We had both found the practice of
meditation significant in life, often meditating together. "I
know," I said to myself. "I need to meditate. Maybe I can
center, calm my muddled thoughts, and make some sense of
all this senseless swirling I am feeling."

Sinking into the couch I closed my eyes, adjusted my posture, said a prayer for Pierre, and began the deep breathing

pattern that had become familiar terrain. I went within myself. Almost immediately Pierre was there, and at last the tears came, numbness lifted by the sight of him in my meditative state. I began to apologize for the misunderstandings that had broken our bond, but quickly he said in my head, "Ssh. Ssh. I see it all differently now."

That began the dialogue of connection that told me once more what I had come to believe with all my heart and mind. Death is just life in another place and the bond isn't broken if we just know how to let it in. Gratefully, I dialogued with someone who had died roughly three thousand miles away, less than twenty-four hours ago, and began the painstaking journey to understand and move into acceptance each of us must take, when someone we care deeply about dies.

Time became a blur for me as it does for others thrust unwillingly into grief. I thought, I am here writing about dying to help others. I didn't realize I'd have my own journey to share as well. Just because I'm writing about death doesn't mean I am immune from experiencing it like everyone else.

Waves of emotion came and went, just as the waves outside my door rhythmically ebbed and flowed against the shore. Shadows deepened. Rich shades of pink and orange managed to penetrate the blur of thoughts that tumbled one upon another. Nighttime was rapidly approaching. Numbness began to give way to short bursts of reason, brief understandings I would have decisions to make, actions to perform. "I'd better have something to eat," I said to myself. "Time to practice what you preach, Joy. Walk the talk of taking care of yourself like you recommend to others."

I had thought in meditation about whether to go home,

interrupt finishing the book to attend the funeral, or to stay in California. "Pierre, what would you want me to do?" I asked.

The answer came clearly and precisely, without hesitation. "I'm fine. All is well here. You understand death is not the end. Stay and finish your work. It is important." The clear acceptance I felt from his energy touching mine was one of his unmistakable presence. I knew his energy, and the feeling I now sensed had the recognizable familiarity of Pierre.

Somehow I made the necessary phone calls. First I phoned Bruce, my son. He lived in California about an hour from Laguna Beach. It was with his help I was here. He assisted me with my computer when I bogged down and reached a technological dead end as well. He was the key to any action I might take, and I knew by now he would be home from work.

"Jan called us, too. She called all three of us, as she wanted to be certain you would get the word. I'm really sorry, Mom. That's a tough call. What can I do to help? You are probably planning to go back for the funeral, aren't you?"

"I don't know, Bruce. I have to sort it all out. It's too soon to know."

"Let me know what you need, and I'll do whatever you need to help." We discussed the possibilities, as I once more grappled with the immediate time ahead. He gave me his work number and I reassured him I would let him know what I decided.

The time difference between East and West Coasts made this the opportune moment for reaching Jan, Pierre's daughter. It was a tearful call, one full of gratitude for her incredible dedication in notifying me and, at the same time, being in touch with the pain of all she had endured and managed in just the past twenty-four hours or less. I desperately wanted to comfort this very caring woman.

Our talk turned to what next, and I felt free to share my clear perception Pierre was urging me to stay in California and finish what I had started. "We talked many times about death. With the work I do it was a natural topic to explore and truthfully, I know your dad was not afraid to die, and believed as I do. Life goes on at a different address in the cosmos. Actually, I can picture he might feel the way it seems to be coming through to me. I may follow that direction." I shared much of the meditation that had helped so much to anchor me.

"Do whatever you feel is right for you. I am fine with that decision. If you change your mind, you're welcome to come, stay here, or whatever I can do to make it easier for you." Her generous and caring spirit touched my heart, and once more the tears came, but this time they were tears of being moved deeply by another's act of kindness.

Kindness is surely what moves the mountain of grief, I thought. How touching that in her sorrow Jan is thinking of me. I've had the kindness of my children and now Jan. It really takes help from others to do this thing called grief.

Next, I called my daughter Carol and shared my process-to-date with her.

"Mom, do you think you are making a mistake? You may want to rethink your decision not to go to the funeral. Pierre might be fine with you staying in California, but I think you may need to go to the funeral for yourself. You only get one opportunity to do that, and I'd hate to see you regret it someday." With a shock I realized her words of wisdom held the ring of truth. I did need to rethink my choices.

I had worried so much about the impact on my children from experiencing so many deaths at such tender ages. There was no way to foretell with certainty the impact on children when death keeps coming as it had for them. First an uncle, then grandparents one at a time, their deaths were an intrusion on the happiness we believe childhood should be. Like every parent I had just done the best I knew how to do, and like every grieving human, some days that had not been nearly good enough.

Now my heart flooded with emotion. All three of my children had been there in support of me, adding their caring, their insight, and offering to help in whatever way I needed. A now-familiar flood of grief swept over me; this time laced with gratitude for the compassion I had just received from those closest to me. They had survived all that early loss and were giving adults able to understand how to help.

Ultimately I found my way. It is really the only choice we have; stay stuck or find a way to deal with it. The persistence of death, demanding that we address it, can't be shirked. It is what is. I began the process of healing.

Long walks on the beach, allowing the rhythms and beauty of nature to touch into my inner reverie, were sandwiched between packing and preparations for leaving. I had decided I needed to go back for the funeral, to reach resolution. Meanwhile the gentle caressing of warm breezes reminded me life went on. Birds still dove and glided. The sunny days full of hope and promise gave warmth to me. The waves ebbed and flowed like the waves of grief that came and went. A time of quiet peace brought another wave that abated.

Nature gave me the understanding it has weathered all

storms and continues to bring beauty, rebirth, endurance, and promise of better days to come. I allowed nature to teach me, remind me of what I knew I needed to recall: Life goes on, finds new rhythms, brings new joys, establishes rebirth and new growth.

"You know what these feelings mean now," I said to myself. "The past has taught you that grief will ultimately end. You will find a way to resolve the waves of emotions. You know something valuable: death never comes to one without a gift in its hand. Look for the gift."

Arrangements were made for me through the helping hands of others. Bruce and Emily made plane reservations. It was Father's Day weekend and the only flight available was Sunday in the very earliest hours. They drove to Laguna Beach and took me home to their house, lovingly nourished my need to be with people who really cared, and tended to my heart and my needs. They fed me great food, and helped me to stay centered and move forward. They gave me the ultimate gift one gives to someone facing a loss from death. They were there for me in any way necessary.

Eventually, I reached home, reorganized my possessions, and drove north to Canada, where there were to be two memorial services: one in the city he lived, and one in the city of his birth where most of his family continued to live.

My loving friends did what wonderful friends do. They met me at the airport, provided safe harbor with places to stay, and accepted where I was at emotionally, which shifted at times from moment to moment. They allowed me to talk and express the changing aspects of grief as they occurred. They saw to it I ate, and my every need was honored.

I was able to speak at both memorial services and honor the genius of a man who had invented purees done in strips,

like Neapolitan ice cream, called Tres Puree, to feed the elderly. They were all natural with beautiful colorings, and
served in an inviting way that changed the nature of a meal
for the elderly to one of excitement with food that nourished and sustained their bodies. I had tasted them and knew
how delicious they were, a gift to a population with very little capacity left to truly enjoy food. It was an honor for me
to share my first-hand knowledge of this invention that lived
on from Pierre's vitality.

I shared with grieving family and friends that I knew
how Pierre felt about dying from our many conversations.
It was a gift to all of us to know he felt peace within that
death is but a new beginning.

Then in time, as we all must, I returned home and went
back to work, both the work of reorganizing my schedule,
energy, emotions and patterns of living, and the work that
paid the bills. I gave myself a little pep talk, "You've watched
people who work with the dying refuse to accept help from
others, believing they must be self reliant when they lose a
loved one. You've heard people say, 'I know, I work in this
business.' Don't let yourself do that. Knowing what is happening is different than feeling it. You must let yourself feel
all of it. Find the way to heal, Joy. You know that one heals
because he chooses to survive. Choose to find the way to
survive and find your way now."

I knew the all too familiar waves of emotion from the
past. Now sadness, anger, resignation, loss, and feelings of
dislocations vied for my attention. I needed to find a way to
move to a newer place of feeling and being. I needed to
reclaim the healthy me who could go forward.

The dolphin workshop seemed a natural choice. I had
been swimming with dolphins before, had experienced the

gentle unconditional love that emanates from their presence. The experiences held magic for me, and joy that was beyond describing. I knew it held potential for my healing unlike anything else I knew. If only I could make my body move through that heavy bogged down feeling that was grief. At the final hour I made the decision, cleared the way and managed to move my slowed down self to arrive for five days at dolphin camp on the Florida Keys. It was almost exactly one month after Pierre's death.

The staff was familiar to me from a previous stay and I shared with them my journey and the need to heal from grief. "I don't want to say anything to others until the end. It isn't fair to intrude on their joyful experience with worry about me," I told them. Two friends of mine also attended the camp, and together we pledged to keep the silence.

Dolphin encounters had been rich with interaction for me in the past. Now the dolphins seemed slightly distant on my swims with them. I knew it was my state of flatness. I had some fluid in my ear and was taking medication for the dizziness. It made me sleepy, subdued, and very unlike my joyous active self. I simply wasn't interesting to the playful dolphins. I decided not to take the medication and see what happened when a more natural me emerged.

The day was ripe with promise. My pod was journeying to a dolphin center to experience dolphins in a natural habitat. All were expectant about the time ahead, except me. I don't know if I'll be able to handle the disappointment if I have no interaction with them, I thought. It is such a loving experience, and I am feeling cheated. I know I'm different than my usual self, but I'm here to heal. Please let that healing begin.

The words of the trainer reached my ears, while I was treading water in the pool. "Make a long line with your arms stretched out, each of you like a T in the water. We'll make a chain and see if the dolphins will swim between you." Dutifully I complied, goggles over my eyes to protect me from the salty water. Nothing seemed to be happening.

Then I saw two dolphin trainers pointing ahead of me and saying, "Look at that. I've never seen them do that." I placed my head in the water to see the object of their awe. Five dolphins were stacked up about twenty feet in front of me, two on top, two on the bottom, and one in the middle, beaming their love at me. Slowly it dawned on me their entire focus was only on me. I felt the waves of energy in my heart for a few impactful minutes, and soon my whole body felt lighter, freer, so light that my legs floated up to the surface. I was unable to hold the T position any longer.

My five dolphins broke rank and began swimming and interacting with all of us. From then on, my freer self returned. The dolphins playfully chased and led me, took me on rides while I held onto their dorsal fins, and brought me the joy only dolphins know how to bring. The magic was back.

For the rest of camp I experienced the wonder and awe I had previously known. I returned home changed by the encounter, further along the trajectory of healing we call-grief work. Five magical loving dolphins had sensed my grief and undertaken to move it. I was deeply touched. That encounter, full of unconditional love and acceptance had changed me. It had required of me only that I stay open to the potential, willing to receive healing in its own time, its own form. From then on I was different.

The whole healing took time, as it always does. There were many challenging moments. Grief didn't disappear, it merely moved over a notch. Time is a healer all by itself. Time augmented by genuine caring, kindness and love from others has the potential to heal the heart. Healing requires we stay open to messages of knowing from unusual places.

The journey of grief, healing through hope and compassion, is highly individual. Each of us must find his or her way.

I believe we are all one. Wherever one of us heals, we change something in the energy for all. The beautiful sadness allows us to see its gifts of tenderness, compassion, and understanding. Our world needs more compassion and more understanding of all that truly matters.

May your journey of hope and compassion continue.

What I Have Learned

Write it on you heart that everyday is the best day in the year.
~ Ralph Waldo Emerson

Something remarkable has happened to me. I, like you, have just read all the stories from *Beautiful Sadness*, and once again I find I am embraced by all the wonder, moments, and poignant emotion that inspired the stories in this book. The people who graced my life, seemingly by chance, brought something magical to my heart and my mind. They shared one common theme: all were determined to make time count instead of counting time, to live as fully as possible while searching to find understanding and make sense of otherwise senseless paths their lives had taken. Our time together shaped my future, forged new viewpoints for me, and taught me what one can only know from living life with others while entwined in deep challenges.

Albert Einstein, who knew a lot about wisdom, perhaps said it best: "Wisdom is not a product of schooling but of the lifelong attempt to achieve it." My special patients spent their last weeks, months, even years—the remaining precious time they had—searching for the meaning of what was happening to them while living as fully as possible every day. The jewels of wisdom and understanding are there for all who earnestly seek to discover. No hierarchy of opportunity is bestowed by birth, wealth, status, or position. No entrance exams must be taken. One must hear the call to action over the cacophony of feelings that strike with startling insistency when tragedy arrives, to find meaning in the otherwise meaningless. The entrance prerequisite is earnest desire to understand how to make life count in whatever form it still exists.

So, just exactly what did I learn? I know without the cognizance of the nightmare we might never do anything significant at all. Try as we might to have a life filled with joy and happiness wherein we can coast and glide, it is the hard times, those poignant moments when we know just how precious life has become, just how dear our special loved ones are to us, are what teach us. These are the moments we can't duck, pray as we might to do so, or hold hidden from our view forever in denial. These are the moments that prompt, if not demand, we undertake a journey of wisdom seeking; we must engage in a spiritual quest of our very own inner truth and meaning.

JOURNEY. What is the journey about? It is a journey, among other emotions, of hope, anticipation, and expectation. What then is the hope about?

Initially, when sudden illness thrusts its presence in our lives we hope it will not be serious. When we seek medical attention and find it is serious, we shift to hoping we will find treatment that will lead to cure. If that hope becomes dashed, we anticipate new avenues of promise that will bring us back to full health.

After all avenues of treatment are exhausted, sometimes after years of earnest effort, we shift to hoping our final time will not be full of degrading pain and suffering. We fervently wish we will be up to the challenge of living our final days with dignity and find the inner peace we so desire. We try not to be a burden to those we love most. Each day we find we earnestly hope something wonderful will happen to help us through that day.

There is, I have come to know, one more shift our hope will make. We move to hoping our lives have made differences to others and we hope we won't be forgotten by those who matter the most to us.

Every time we let someone we love and care about know we will never forget the wonderful times we shared, and will always carry part of that loved one in our heart, we feed the final hope that sustains the person preparing to die. We give that other person a precious gift of knowing his or her final hope has come true.

Hope reshaped, reformed, and restored becomes a rich and powerful ongoing force that liberates our spirits and our senses of dignity. For the ill or dying person hope is the pivotal and essential tool for making each day count.

Sadly, too often hope has become an act of desperation in our society. We hope when we feel there is nothing else we can do. "Things are so desperate all I can do is hope." In actuality, hope, when coupled with anticipation and expectation, becomes a viable force for living. First we hope for an outcome. Then we must anticipate it is possible to achieve our hope, and be able to picture some of how it would be to experience. Expectation that it can be achieved completes the triumvirate for action. For where is the action in hoping for something we fail to anticipate as possible or expect to come into our reality? Hope, stripped of anticipation or expectation, becomes weak and ineffectual.

Hope, anticipation, and expectation are generating energies that assist the probable to become possible, and the possible to finally move into actual. Hope, sustained by anticipation and expectation, can be the heart of this most important journey.

If hope is the heart of the journey, then support, forgiveness, compassion, and acceptance are its steadfast companions. Let me talk briefly about each.

SUPPORT is what we all long for and desperately need to believe will be there for us in our time of need. But what does it encompass?

Support—and what it represents—changes from person to person. Basically it means someone will be there for me in a way I find acceptable, to understand, to accept me on days that are not so good and far from my best, and to love me anyway. It means there is an oasis of understanding to which I can retreat for solace, to refuel, to renew my energy, my sense of dignity, and my hope. How that translates into action has everything to do with the personalities and relationships involved.

No perfect formulas for support can be pulled out and faithfully adhered to in times of crises. Support is both physical—meals, laundry, housekeeping, running errands—and emotional—caring, understanding, visiting, listening and being there. Support can be so simple and so profound as just sitting with hand outstretched silently holding the hand of the other.

Wordless support is powerful beyond what words can describe. Never question the impact of just being present helping to share the moment. I have watched the revival that happens, observing energy being transferred to the one in crisis right before my eyes. Experience has taught me that energy, and caring willingly given, energize the giver as well as the receiver. I have heard over and over from patients that "you find who your friends really are when you are sick and dying." The catch in providing support is to avoid resentment, or the feeling of having to, which can evolve into martyrdom, that can accompany giving to a very needy human, even when we love him/her deeply.

A much-quoted philosophy tells us that no man is an island. For years I have said, I am not even a peninsula. To know we have limits is strength, not weakness. We are called to have boundaries that protect ourselves even in the crucial moments of giving to the ones we love the most. Each of us is called to realize, understand, and know within our hearts and minds, we cannot be all things to anyone, let alone everyone. It is easy to wake up and find ourselves entrapped by the giving and caring that felt so right when we generously gave from hearts filled with love.

Think for a moment about a well of water. We can all see that giving out water from the well while cutting off the underground source of water is a surefire prescription for the well to run dry. Think of yourself as a well and recognize you can only continue to give out what you are willing to replenish within your inner being.

One of the most significant moves we can make is to allow others to support us as we care-take our loved ones. This is the time to dialogue with friends, volunteers, nurses, counselors, and helping hands to shore up our own inner strength by allowing support to reach and nourish us.

Support offers growth to all who are involved in facing death, when we allow it to enrich our understanding and our ability to know and live life more deeply, more fully and with the wisdom that is born out of experiences. I urge you to empower yourself to reach out and receive support as well as to give it. The journey of support need never be made alone.

FORGIVENESS is a conscious choice made which can liberate us from a lifetime of pain transforming us to a glorious place of healing, joy, and peace.

Forgiveness is a choice so significant, powerful, and life changing. We marvel at the impact we feel whenever we witness the power of forgiving.

Just why, then, is forgiveness so hard to achieve? What holds us back from what can be ours to experience if we forgive another?

Perhaps our largest stumbling block is a belief someone forgiven got away with what happened "scot-free." "I had to suffer and he/she got away with it, with no price to pay," we say. We fail to recognize that each of us must stand and face what we have done, said, and who we have been, at our times of death. There is no "scot-free" for anyone's actions, no matter how it may seem.

"For whose sake do I forgive another?" Some would say for God's sake, others for the sake of my soul, or to ensure we have God's love. But God's love for us is unconditional. He loves us anyway. God is not harmed by our unforgiveness. We are.

The simple truth is we forgive another for our own sake's. That may or may not help another. It does help us. Learning self-love, although difficult, is the key. Forgiveness breaks imprisoning emotional bonds and lets us off the hook from the negative thoughts that play constantly in our heads, thoughts that drive us deeper and farther away from the truer version of the self we can become.

Forgiving another is a gift of caring we give ourselves when we love ourselves enough to become all we can be in this life. The ultimate question becomes, "Do I love myself enough to forgive another, and then forgive myself for drawing this to me, and for my part in it?" The gift we receive is the ability to be more of our truer selves. Suddenly everything is different.

I invite you to love yourself enough to forgive for your sake. There is a more wonderful you just waiting to be set free once you care enough to do so.

COMPASSION may be the most elusive part of the journey to understand. For compassion is genuine caring born from feeling the sorrow of others, and truly feeling that sorrow within our hearts, minds, and inner selves. What does sorrow encompass?

Sorrow is the sadness we feel about things we can do nothing about. Compassion is the genuine feeling that another is locked into sorrow, and knowing he/she truly is immersed in sorrow we allow ourselves to feel the sadness, too.

Compassion is a level of caring beyond pity, sympathy, and empathy. By now we know, from the explorations of science, all thoughts and feelings send energy to others as silent messages that are either strong or weak. Pity and sympathy, with their feeling sorry for another, send messages of weakness to the other. They are messages we feel better than the "poor" one we pity. Although pity and sympathy are natural emotions to experience, we must be clear we choose to move through them to more positive ways of viewing any situation.

Empathy moves us to a higher feeling of knowing, one that allows us to feel this could be me, and to reach a high-er level of understanding. Positive support flows from feelings of empathy as we reach a point of leveling the playing field. It could be either of us, and this is sad.

Compassion brings caring, born of tenderness, love, and sorrow, and it provides the matrix within which all involved can grow and reach to new heights of achievement.

Compassion provides the glue, the substance, the web of caring that holds and protects another from the disintegration of their self-pity. "Someone sees how this is and I am no longer alone seeing how awful and overwhelming my life has become." Compassion allows us to carry part of the emotional load and speaks a message of acceptance to another that reaches beyond words. It is undeniably powerful to receive, and feeling compassion allows movement for the giver that is beyond expectation.

Compassion can allow an easier transition into strength and peace. The Dalai Lama, who has raised compassion to a new level for our awareness to see and model, said it beautifully, "Compassion and love are not mere luxuries. As the source of both inner and external peace, they are fundamental to the continued survival of our species."

Why then do we sidestep compassion and stay in the more superficial level of sympathy? Compassion is viewed by some as a sign of weakness that reduces one to wallowing in emotion for the sadness that exists in life. Some people fear becoming stuck in all of the sadness. "What if I can't pull back from feeling the sorrow? I must run from all this sadness before I become a sympathetic push-over," they reason. In this instance compassion has been confused with pity and sympathy, which does convey a weak energy.

Eleanor Roosevelt, who learned a great deal about compassion, offered us this analysis, "Too many of us stay walled up because we are afraid of being hurt. We are afraid to care too much, for fear that the other person does not care at all."

Some feel there is so much sadness and sorrow in the world they will surely break under the weight of it all. It is not that we must feel all the sorrow. It is required of us that we know and realize others feel the sorrow of their lives and are impacted by that sadness. Compassion allows us to move into acceptance that unresolved sadness is the cause of many of the behaviors and attitudes that run unfettered in our world.

To reach a level of compassion, we must first allow ourselves to feel sorrow, consciously turn to the sadness we know, sadness about things we can do nothing about. As we feel genuinely sorry life couldn't have been different, and allow ourselves to forgive others and ourselves for the aspects we can never change, something magical begins to happen. Tenderness creeps in coupled with new understanding. Our first compassion must be for ourselves, as we feel it actively and begin to shift our perspectives and perceptions. We see that we know more now and would do it differently, or we see that life must be taken as it unfolds so then we allow ourselves to begin the move beyond the urge to withdraw and retreat. We see that co-existing with the sadness is knowledge we could only have gained from experience. Allowing ourselves compassion that we did what we knew to do at the time, allowing ourselves to feel genuinely sorry, then moving to feeling the tenderness towards self within us, starts the journey of self to forge new hope and dignity. We move towards wisdom.

The move to feeling tenderness and caring for others can then be made more easily. Now we are free to see that beyond life's sadness is also beauty, joy, and happiness—feelings now heightened by contrast and made all the more precious for realizing their significance anew. We open to igniting our passion to do what we can do, even if that is to hold the energy in loving support for another. We move beyond needing to fix the problem to being there, allowing the caring of our presence to matter.

Compassion and love are our hopes for the future. Compassion and love, combined with hope and forgiveness, raise the bar on what we can achieve in the journey to live our best lives and to be meaningfully in support of those we love most.

ACCEPTANCE. How do we ever reach acceptance? How do we learn to accept the unacceptable? "Ah, there's the rub. With great difficulty," I hear you saying.

It is difficult, and at times overwhelmingly impossible, to learn to accept the finality of what has happened and cannot be changed. The journey from the devastation that has occurred to hope for the life that could be, seems a long, arduous trip to take. We wonder in all sincerity if it is possible to learn to accept the unacceptable.

Shock, denial, disbelief, resentment, and a sense of abject despair must be endured, waded through, and rejected as a course for which we settle in order for us to come out the other side of the nightmare. One by one we try, and must reject, the paths that cannot be denied before we see their futility. We worry we will never be able to be happy again. We doubt that life will ever be the same, question we are losing our sanity as we can no longer think straight, despair there is a future out there for us. We begin to see we can't change the past, but we can ruin the present by worrying over the future.

Sometimes our strength allows us to be strong and seemingly in control early in the grieving period, only to find weeks and months later we have the equivalent of not being able to get out of bed. How could I not see how I really felt about this loss? we wonder. Who did I think I was fooling? Usually the answer is only myself.

There is no substitute for time to deal with the many aspects of loss. One can never rush the realization in another's journey, nor can we rush our own. It takes time, way too much time it seems, to learn what is just is. We must learn to deal with is-ness.

That includes learning to understand and accept the many distasteful stages unfolding as a necessary part of the process.

When someone we love is critically ill or dies, we are powerless to change the event. We may have no choice (not even small choices) in the outcome, and we can't make it go away. The only point of power we have is how we view the event. We must change our perceptions and our perspectives.

We fail to see we have locked tightly the door on the prison of our unrest by being unwilling to let go of energy that entraps us. Slowly it dawns on us, we are both jailer and prisoner by virtue of our thoughts.

The journey to acceptance begins with choice. "I choose to find a way. I don't know what that is and I am doing it anyway." This choice, so often feeling like a last resort, is really the first step. When we choose to find the way we fire our right use of will. Our courage can then come forth. Courage is not the opposite of weakness. Courage is going forward and doing something anyway—even when we aren't sure how—because we choose to find an appropriate and successful way.

Diane de Poitiers offers us an insightful viewpoint on courage. "Courage is as often the outcome of despair as of hope; in the one case we have nothing to lose, in the other everything to gain."

Time is the helping hand for both choice and courage. What I have learned is we must make our choices over and over many times. When we feel despair returning we choose again and again "to find the way. I don't know how I'm doing this but I choose to do it." Choice, pure determined choice to survive, is the ultimate power tool we need in our arsenal. People who have survived tragedy, crises, illness, and loss all have in common one aspect: they kept choosing to make it until they did.

One door leads to another in life. We must remember there are many paths to the same outcome. We must be willing to forgo the seemingly easy route of a formula for success, for the personal search that allows us to open one door, go to another and yet another, until our own paths unfold.

Support of others, forgiveness of ourselves and others, hope, compassion, and acceptance all come together in their own special blend for our lives. In the final analysis, we are not talking about dying. We are really talking about living through the illness, making every day count, through the grief, and into the life that lies ahead of each of us.

To the dandelion, the fluffy white bloom would seem to be the end of its life, if it could think like we do. The dandelion might feel it was all over, never to be again. We recognize the truth; the fluffy white seeds fly away to become new points of life, and the cycle starts anew. They are really like the seeds of love that come from someone we have loved who has crossed over into the next stage of life. One or more seeds of life, given to each recipient, live on in the hearts and minds of all who knew that person and allowed their lives to be touched by them.

There can be beauty to the sadness, with its tenderness, hope, and compassion.

The journey that cannot be shirked is ultimately worth taking with courage, compassion for self and others, renewed hope, acceptance, and the support of others. I wish you a rewarding journey and send you forth with an Irish blessing as you go on your way.

May the road rise to meet you,

May the wind always be at your back,

May the sun shine warm upon your face

May the rains fall softly upon your fields.

I will add to that: May you find the beauty that is interwoven with sadness.

"To laugh often and much, to win the respect of intelligent people and the affection of children, to earn the appreciation of honest critics and endure the betrayal of false friends, to appreciate beauty, to find the best in others, to leave the world a bit better, whether by a healthy child, a garden patch...to know even one life has breathed easier because you have lived. This is to have succeeded!" wrote Ralph Waldo Emerson.